RELIGIONS IN AMERICA

edited by HERBERT L. MARX, JR.

THE REFERENCE SHELF
Volume 49   Number 6

THE H. W. WILSON COMPANY
New York   1977

THE REFERENCE SHELF

The books in this series contain reprints of articles, excerpts from books, and addresses on current issues and social trends in the United States and other countries. There are six separately bound numbers in each volume, all of which are generally published in the same calendar year. One number is a collection of recent speeches; each of the others is devoted to a single subject and gives background information and discussion from various points of view, concluding with a comprehensive bibliography. Books in the series may be purchased individually or on subscription.

Library of Congress Cataloging in Publication Data
Main entry under title:

Religions in America.

(The Reference shelf ; v. 49, no. 6)
Bibliography: p.
1. United States—Religion—1945–   —Addresses, essays, lectures. I. Marx, Herbert L. II. Series.

BL2530.U6R43   200'.973   77–16142
ISBN 0-8242-0608-8

PREFACE

There is no subject more important than religion. It involves the most fateful questions, to which different religions give different answers. The way religion has usually been taught, from Sunday school to college, one might hardly notice that. As a result, many, if not most, people who have gone to universities know scarcely anything about religion. They may say that it is, of course, very important, but they obviously feel that it can be safely ignored. I feel that those who close their eyes to the great religions are thoughtless and, in effect, refuse to think about alternative answers to some of the most crucial questions.—Walter Kaufmann, *Religions in Four Dimensions.*

To undertake in one small volume a study of religions, even if confined to the United States, is a challenging task. The diversity and depth of the subject, the particular viewpoints and lifelong beliefs that any reader brings to it, make the project insurmountable—unless strict limitations as to scope are followed.

Such limitations should therefore be expressed at the outset. First of all, this volume is not encyclopedic in nature. No attempt is made to survey all the religions in America. The major religious divisions—Catholicism, Protestantism, and Judaism—are, of course, discussed in these pages. But beyond this, example must suffice. Among religions *not* discussed are Catholic and Orthodox churches other than the Roman Catholic Church, and significant American religious groups such as the Jehovah's Witnesses. Some of the "new" religions, largely drawn from Asia, are mentioned, but others are omitted for lack of space (Zen Buddhism is an example). The Society for Ethical Culture is not treated, although a selection is included by one of its leaders. Two black religions are included; many others are not.

A second limitation is that this volume treats sparingly the concepts of theology—aspects of the belief in God as con-

ceived by various religions. The sole exception here is
contained in Section II in the selections dealing with the
Hartford and Boston Affirmations.

What *is* included is a survey of religions in America, with
emphasis on the changes and developments that have taken
place in recent years. The basic purpose of the book is to
emphasize the extraordinary number of religious "happenings" in the United States today. Some are interrelated and
some stand on their own. Among those considered in sections of this book are the following:

☐ A resurgence of evangelicalism—a personal enthusiasm and transformation said to be experienced by growing
numbers of Americans (Section II)

☐ An unusually strong degree of affiliation of young
people in many new types of religion, as well as an apparent
upswing in their attention to traditional forms of religion
(Section V)

☐ Changes in the Roman Catholic Church, by no means
confined to the United States, since the Second Vatican
Council of 1962–1965—which was characterized by the
modernizing and liberalizing of many of the Church's practices and attitudes (Section III)

☐ An interest in the relationship between politics and
religion—under a Constitution that prohibits any law "respecting an establishment of religion"—with a President of
the United States openly avowing his deep attachment to
and support of his religious faith and principles (Section II)

Among all Americans, over 60 percent claim affiliation
with some form of organized religion. Among the major
American religious bodies (including their membership) are
the following: Protestant, including various Latter-Day
Saints (Mormon) groups and the Jehovah's Witnesses, 71
million; Roman Catholic, 49 million; Jewish, 6 million;
Eastern Orthodox, 4 million; and Islamic, 3 million.

The authors of many of the selections reprinted in this
volume stress the relationship between developments in religion and the general conditions of life in the United States
today. Some would argue that spiritual matters may stand

apart, unrelated to worldly matters. Yet others note that religious belief and practice are significantly affected by such considerations as lifestyles; the pervasive influence of the mass media, especially television; the women's movement; and new attitudes toward marriage and sexual relationships. It is these considerations, among others, that are recurring themes in this compilation.

Section I broadly discusses the place of religion in the United States today. Sections II and III examine the Protestant and Roman Catholic faiths, respectively, while Section IV deals with a variety of religions. The next two sections treat the subject of youth and religion: Section V details some of the religious activity of young America; Section VI views the status of religious education. The future of both traditional religious and new movements in this country is the subject of this volume's final section.

The editor expresses sincere appreciation to the authors, publishers, organizations, and publications that have granted permission to include the materials that make up this volume. Special acknowledgment is also made to the New York Public Library, particularly the research facilities of the Mid-Manhattan branch.

HERBERT L. MARX, JR.

November 1977

CONTENTS

I. THE CHANGING ROLE OF RELIGIONS

EDITOR'S INTRODUCTION

Before we examine the diversity and changing nature of particular religious beliefs and organizational structures, some observations on the general place of all religious activity in the United States today are necessary. As noted by many of the commentators throughout this volume, the 1970s have seen much turmoil, uplift, and expansion in religious activity.

Periods of rapid and turbulent change are not new or unprecedented, however, as the first selection, from *Editorial Research Reports,* notes. In the next selection, Leo Rosten, author of *The Religions of America: Faith and Ferment in a Time of Crisis,* catalogs the evidence of changes occurring today.

George Gallup, Jr., presents in the next article sweeping statistical evidence of a "profound religious revival" occurring in the United States today. Philosophy professor Walter Kaufmann, however, offers some cautionary advice concerning the extent of this revival, and in fact expresses doubt as to the validity of some of Gallup's findings.

The role religion plays in the general structure of our society is touched upon in this section's final extract—observations by sociology professor Peter Berger on the strong links between religion's "spiritual crisis" and the quality of life in America today.

THE HISTORICAL SETTING [1]

The current mood of reflection, reassessment and prayer brings major churches to a new phase in a long-standing

[1] From "Year of Religion," by Helen B. Shaffer, staff writer. *Editorial Research Reports.* v2, no 8:569–74. Ag. 8, '75. Reprinted by permission.

dual development of liberal and conservative tendencies in the religious life of the nation. The churches have at times been a force for social reform, at other times a bulwark of the status quo. Often the two tendencies have caused conflicts and rifts within a single denominational body.

The early American colonists were often religious dissidents, and they in turn bred dissidents in their own ranks. Over the years churches divided not only over doctrine but over social and political matters, usually in a moral context. Sectional interests separated Christian bodies well before the climactic splits of the Civil War; differences developed not only between North and South but between the urban East and the frontier West. . . .

Flowering of Social Gospel After the Civil War

The church in America has had its periods of quiescence and its periods of upheaval. The post-Civil War period was a time of relative placidity and steady growth, when church membership and regular church attendance were becoming established as the norm of the American middle class. This period also saw the flowering of the Social Gospel, the appearance of a succession of fiery evangelists and a certain fringe growth of cults, usually with an Eastern orientation. But the main line of Protestant development continued to support a stable institutionalized structure for each church body. In its doctrines, rituals, hymns and modes of devotional exercise, each denomination tended to reflect not only the shared Christian heritage but the distinctive way-of-life, social deportment and mind-set of its particular constituency.

Relative quiescence and identification of organized religion with its secular setting were healthy for church growth. From an estimated 6 per cent of the population in 1776, church membership grew, thanks partly to frontier evangelism, to 15.5 per cent by 1850. The churches a half-century later could count one-third of the population as members. The proportion rose to more than 50 per cent by the mid-1920s and reached two-thirds during the 1950s.

Both Protestant and Catholic membership growth benefited from "immigration, evangelism, the appeals of the churches and the habits of the nation."

Meanwhile, the preachings of the Social Gospel were having a lasting effect on mainline Protestantism. The notion that the gospel commanded good Christians to seek to undo injustices inflicted by an indifferent society on the poor, the weak and the oppressed began to permeate theological discourse and then to influence policies of major churches. The Social Gospel was given formal approval in a social creed adopted in 1908 by the Federal Council of Churches, forerunner of the present National Council of Churches of Christ in the United States.

What became known as Social Christianity subsided somewhat during the 1920s for several reasons. For one, it called forth a counter-movement on the part of fundamentalist churches, which formed their own federation and pressed their influence for conservative social and theological positions. The contest between Fundamentalism and Modernism was impressed on the nation during the famous Scopes trial of 1925, when an obscure biology teacher in Tennessee was charged with the offense of teaching Darwin's theory of evolution in defiance of a state law forbidding the teaching in public schools of anything contrary to the biblical story of creation.

In addition, social action for labor reforms was kept at bay during the 1920s by the "red scare"—the fear of rampant Bolshevism and anarchy. It put the taint of radicalism on anyone who supported trade unionism. The pulpit in the 1920s rang out with more denunciations of pool halls and Hollywood morals than tirades against the exploitation of the working man.

The social reforms of the New Deal could be considered a victory for Social Christianity. Together with the economic crisis of the 1930s, the social-minded churches helped make support of labor unionization and abolition of child labor respectable moral positions. Meanwhile, the rise of Hitler and the growing military strength of Nazi Germany were eroding pacifism, a byproduct of the earlier Social Christian movement. World War II muted the issues that split Christian America on modern-progressive or conservative-fundamentalist lines. Then the end of the war initiated a new period of placidity in the religious life of the nation.

This was the era of Norman Vincent Peale's *Power of Positive Thinking,* Bishop Fulton Sheen's *Peace of Soul* and Billy Graham's *Peace with God,* all best-sellers, as was Rabbi Joshua Loth Liebman's *Peace of Mind.* Some critical voices were raised to complain that the church was becoming too complacent, the religious message too soothing. Increased church attendance, they argued, was not necessarily a sign of growing faith but perhaps a reflection of the growth of the middle class and adoption by newcomers to that class of the social habits expected of them.

Upheavals and Radical Theology in the Sixties

Religion in America began to churn up again toward the end of the 1950s with the first stirrings of the civil rights movement. The example of Martin Luther King Jr. helped stir the conscience of his fellow ministers in white communities. Before long it was taken for granted that the clergy, black and white, Protestant, Catholic, and Jewish, would be in the lead in the marches, the picketing and the mass rallies for the rights of black citizens and for related social goals.

For reasons not yet entirely clear to historians and sociologists of religion, the decade of the 1960s also marked a sudden popularization of a radical theology that some took so far as to proclaim the death of God. Radical theology came forward in an atmosphere created by a sense that change was the preeminent factor in modern life. The world was changing, therefore religion should change with it. The focus of religion in the future was not to be the mysterious other world but the only world that man knew—the one he lived in.

The new theology fitted in with an era when Americans responded—favorably or otherwise—to the drama of priests, ministers and rabbis marching openly in defiance of civil authorities to protest injustice in the name of the Lord. For it was a decade of turmoil, of assassinations of popular heroes and disillusionment with non-violent protest, of mounting racial tensions and riots, of generational cleavages and divisiveness over the U.S. military involvement in Vietnam. As in the past, turmoil in the social and political sphere spilled over into the religious. . . .

Radical theology became popularized with the publication of a number of books on the subject that were widely read. Much of this theology was built on the philosophy of Dietrich Bonhoeffer, a German Lutheran pastor martyred by the Nazis, as set forth in his *Letters and Papers from Prison*, published posthumously in the United States in 1953, and other writings. Bonhoeffer stressed the need to develop a secular application of scripture.

The general trend of the new theology was away from the elements of mystery and the supernatural and toward the mundane. Some of the new theologians felt it was time for man to work out his own religious destiny on earth without help of a deity. "Contemporaneous with this development, and closely related to it, was a veritable tidal wave of questioning of all the traditional structures of Christendom, above all, the so-called 'parish' church. . . . The ministry and laity alike have shown an increasingly widespread tendency to regard local church structures as irrelevant, or as extremely unadaptable to the most urgent needs of the times, or even as an impediment to social action" [according to writer Sydney E. Ahlstrom].

Developments Stemming from Vatican Council

Still another major contribution to the upheavals in organized religion during the 1960s was Vatican II, which affected not only the Catholic church but encouraged the impulse for change and modernization of nearly all aspects of major Protestant denominations as well. The purpose of this historic conclave first announced by Pope John XXIII in 1959, was to review and consider modernization of nearly all aspects of Catholicism. Only basic dogma was not to be tampered with. But most other areas—theology, polity, morals, structure, the role of laity and clergy, the liturgy, relations with other churches, rules for family relations, religious education—were up for reform.

Among developments emanating from Vatican II cited by an official Catholic source are: more interfaith contact and collaboration; more participation by laity, especially women, in the church mission; "a new attentiveness to the 'signs of the times' as indicators of needed directions of ministry"; sweeping liturgical changes; loss of members of the clergy and religious orders; more sharing of responsibility among different levels of hierarchy and with lay councils; and a "considerable change" in theology without change of doctrine.

FERMENT IN THE CHURCHES [2]

Our churches are in as much turmoil as our political institutions. Both are caught in a revolution of our moral and ethical codes. Consider these dramatic facts, chosen at random:

☐ About 75 percent of the American people think "religion is losing its influence."

☐ Only 50 percent of Roman Catholics attend church during an average week, and only 37 percent of Protestants attend.

☐ An official commission of 26 Roman Catholic and Lutheran theologians has concluded that "papal primacy" need no longer be a "barrier to reconciliation" between their churches. This may prove to be the most historic event in Lutheranism since Martin Luther nailed his astounding manifesto to the door of All Saints church in Wittenberg.

☐ In Philadelphia four bishops of the Episcopal church defied their superiors and were present when 11 women—

[2] From "Ferment in Our Churches," by Leo Rosten, author, economist, and political scientist. *Saturday Review*.2:6 Jl. 12, '75. Reprinted by permission.

the first in the history of the church—were ordained as Episcopal priests.

☐ The birthrate among Catholics is rapidly declining and will soon approach the birthrate for Protestants and Jews.

☐ Of the Catholic women polled, 83 percent oppose the Vatican's strict ban on the use of "artificial" birth-control devices; 37 percent stated that they use the contraceptive Pill; fewer than one-third use the rhythm method recommended by the church.

☐ The Episcopal church has so liberalized its position on divorce that excommunication is no longer imposed on those who ignore the church's earlier requirement that a remarriage be judged and approved by a bishop.

☐ The Rabbinical Assembly, representing Conservative Judaism, has voted to "count" women henceforth for a *minyan*—the minimum number of adults (10) needed for communal worship. . . .

☐ Roman Catholics, asked whether a divorced Catholic who remarries is "living in sin," responded: no, 60 percent; yes, 28 percent; don't know, 12 percent.

☐ In 1972, 67 percent of the adult American public approved of marriages between Christians and Jews. (In 1968, 59 percent held this view.)

☐ Deacons of the Roman Catholic Church may now be laymen—a revival of the ancient form of Christian ministry. Within the past year, 13 laymen in the New York archdiocese have been ordained as deacons and have presided over weddings.

The ferment within Roman Catholicism is perhaps the most dramatic (and surely the most publicized) revelation of the rebellion agitating our religious orders. Consider these highlights from a survey of American Catholics over 17 years of age:

☐ Over a third do not attend Sunday mass regularly.

☐ Two-thirds have not gone to confession within the preceding two months.

☐ Over two-thirds predict that the church will have to abandon its disapproval of divorce.

☐ One-half favor a relaxation of the church's prohibition of abortions.

☐ Less than 10 percent of the Catholic laity think that their children will "lose their souls" if they leave the church.

☐ Sixty-four percent of Roman Catholic *priests* under 40 disagree with the Vatican's ban on the use of "artificial devices" for birth control.

☐ A Gallup Poll estimates that 2,500 Catholic priests are "dropping out" each year.

☐ Among *priests* 39 years old and younger, 77 percent hold that priests should be allowed to marry; 52 percent of all priests polled agreed.

☐ Almost 80 percent of the Roman Catholic laity polled in 1974 favor allowing priests to marry.

☐ Almost a third of American Catholics would support the ordination of women as priests.

☐ "Should priests who marry be excommunicated?" The Catholic clergy responded: no, 60 percent—and 79 percent of those 39 years old and younger.

☐ Of white Catholics, only 21 percent said they would respect a "priest's exhortation" to integrate their neighborhoods; 46 percent would refuse Holy Communion from a black priest.

However I interpret this mass of hard data, I cannot help concluding that the fortresses of faith are experiencing the most profound alterations in centuries. Church authority is being challenged on a dozen fronts. Traditional creeds are being drastically revised. Hallowed canons are being shelved. Religious practices are changing daily. Church leaders are beleaguered by new, bold, persistent demands—from their clergy no less than from their congregations.

It is not hyperbole to say that we are witnessing a remarkable erosion of consensus within the citadel of belief. What prophet, what theologian, what historian or scholar could have predicted the militant participation of clergymen in civil-rights marches, the presence at Catholic altars of Protestant and Jewish clergymen during marriage ceremonies, the "God is Dead" debate, the open campaign of homosexuals against anathematization, the mounting skepticism about the validity or effectiveness of church teachings, the growth of "charismatic" groups and interfaith communes, the phenomena of "jazz masses" and rock-and-roll music in cathedrals . . . ?

We are in the eye of a storm. The velocity and power of that storm should surprise the most sophisticated observers.

"PROFOUND RELIGIOUS REVIVAL" [3]

Evidence is mounting that the U.S. may be in an early stage of a profound religious revival, with the Evangelical movement providing a powerful thrust.

In terms of what might be described as "hard" evidence, the Gallup Poll has recorded a rise in church attendance for 1976 for the first time in nearly two decades, with 42 percent of Americans attending church or synagogue in a typical week. Our surveys also show church *membership* to be on the upswing during the year with about 7 in 10 now describing themselves as church members. Another barometer which has measured swings in religiousness—both in terms of organizational and non-organizational religion—is one which asks each person the importance of religion in his or her life. This barometer also indicates a trend upward, with about 6 in 10 saying their religious beliefs are "very important" in their lives. These gains for religion have been accompanied by considerable interest on the part of the public in what might be termed "experiential religion" —involvement in such movements as Transcendental Meditation, Yoga, the Charismatic Movement, Mysticism and Eastern religions. A recent survey which we conducted indicates that a projected 6 million Americans are participating

[3] From "U.S. in Early Stage of Religous Revival?" by George Gallup Jr., president, American Institute of Public Opinion. *Journal of Current Social Issues.* 14:50–5. Spring '77. Reprinted by permission.

in, or are involved in TM, 5 million in Yoga, 3 million in the Charismatic Movement (Charismatic Renewal), 3 million in Mysticism, and 2 million in Eastern religions. [See "Transcendental Meditation," in Section IV, below.]

It is important to note that interest in these movements is not necessarily in conflict with organized religion and, in fact, is often supportive, with considerable experimentation found among church members.

The *observations* of both laity and clergy as well as behavioral measurements, indicate an upturn in religious interest and activity.

A recent Gallup survey of U.S. adults showed that the proportion who believe religion is increasing its influence on American life is up sharply in recent months and has tripled since 1971. The observations of clergy and other religious leaders would also seem to point in this direction. I have had occasion in recent weeks to talk to religious leaders of many faiths and denominations and they are in general agreement that there is a deeper search for non-material values and a renewed interest in religion.

Evangelical leaders appear to be the most convinced that there is evidence of renewed religious zeal. And, indeed, Gallup Poll findings show the Evangelical movement in this nation to be an increasingly powerful one, affecting the religious character of many churches. A widely reported Gallup Poll finding last summer showed 1 person in 3 (34 percent) saying he or she has been "born again"—that is, has had a turning point in life of commitment to Jesus Christ. In terms of numbers, this figure represents nearly 50 million Americans, 18 and over. Among Protestants alone, nearly half (48 percent) say they are "born again" Christians, which represents some 43 million adults. One way of defining an Evangelical would be a person who (1) has had a "born again" experience, (2) holds a literal interpretation of the Bible (or accepts its absolute authority), and (3) witnesses to his or her faith. Of the total national sample, 1 in 5 meets all three tests. Among the various factors which could be pointed to as accounting for the increased activity in the religious and spiritual climate of the U.S. are the following:

A turning inward to seek refuge from the pressures of everyday existence.

A search for non-material values in light of the disappointments of the material world and the fading of the "American dream."

President Carter's open discussion of his own personal religious beliefs, which has focused new attention on religion in the U.S. and particularly the Evangelical movement.

A normal upswing following a decline in religious interest and activity. In broad terms, America's religious scene has historically been characterized by periods of religious zeal followed by a drift back to religious apathy. Thus there was a sharp upswing in religious interest and participation in the late 1950s, a downward trend during the late 1960s (primarily among Catholics), a leveling off during the first years of the 1970s and now, apparently, another upturn.

The efforts of the nation's clergy in response to the need to make religion more appealing to young people and to satisfy their apparent spiritual hunger.

While the growth in religious interest and activity appears to be across-the-board in terms of population groups, it is centered largely among young adults, where the sharpest gains are recorded, not only in church attendance and membership but also in the proportion saying religion plays an important role in their lives. Thus, what many religious leaders had fervently hoped would happen now may be occurring: young people, after having expressed their disenchantment in the 1960s with the Establishment, including organized religion, now, in the mid and late 1970s, are moving back into the ranks of church members. Survey findings presented here would seem to offer solid evidence that

Americans are religiously healthy. In addition, a recently-completed 70-nation survey, conducted for the Charles F. Kettering Foundation by Gallup International Research Institutes, shows the U.S. to be the most religious nation of the world among the advanced nations surveyed. Even in the face of these findings one must nevertheless ask: Are we really as religious as we appear? Are we perhaps only *superficially* religious? Indeed America appears to be facing a seeming paradox: religion is *increasing* its influence on society but morality is *losing* its influence. The secular world would seem to offer abundant evidence that religion is not greatly affecting our lives. The U.S. has one of the worst records in the world in terms of criminal victimization. We live in a "ripoff" society and every day we read of consumer fraud, political corruption, tax cheating, bribery, payoffs and so forth.

Yet one could argue that the reports of crime and immorality in the U.S. would be far *worse* if religion did not in some fashion enter the lives of most of us. In fact, a study conducted for the Miami Valley Young Adult Ministry, Inc. on the "attitudes, values and life-styles" of young adults in Greater Dayton (Ohio) suggests the strong influence religious faith can have on lives, in terms of restraint, as well as in terms of guidance and inspiration.

The Dayton study, as well as numerous other studies, have also clearly indicated that religiously-oriented youth are happier, more confident in their futures and less inclined to use drugs and alcohol to excess than are youth who are *not* religiously-oriented.

Religious motivation also helps explain the current explosion in volunteerism in the U.S. One out of every 4 people, 14 years of age and older, volunteers time to some non-profit organization. Over 50 percent of this volunteer time is given to churches and synagogues.

While religion is clearly playing an important role in our lives, some religious leaders feel that much of the new interest in religion is sheer emotionalism—a temporary "high"—and question whether there is anything of substance to this religious zeal. And few religious leaders, of course, would be satisfied with evidence of merely *numerical* gains —filling up the pews. Obviously the ultimate goal for Christianity is to deepen religious faith and commitment. New survey efforts are being made to explore in greater depth the religious climate of the nation. One of the key measurements to be developed might be one to determine the level of "religious maturity." While Americans may be impressively religious in terms of outward manifestations, survey evidence indicates a wide gap between belief and practice. In addition, the prayer life of many might be considered rudimentary and underdeveloped. Surveys reveal a shocking lack of knowledge regarding certain basic facts about the doctrines and history of our own churches. Perhaps religious faith to many is merely supportive and not challenging: are our churches producing "nice" people or "new" people? . . .

Time will tell whether America is on a religious "kick" or whether we are indeed becoming a more religiously committed nation. The shape of the future depends to a considerable extent on the religious beliefs, practices and expectations of two key groups in society—the college-educated, who include a high proportion of the opinion leaders among the public, and the young, who will set the tone for the church and for the nation in the years ahead.

While it is generally assumed that the more formal education one has the less religious he or she becomes, this does not appear to be the case for Americans. The 70-nation study referred to earlier shows the U.S. to be unique in that we have *both* a high level of formal education and display a high level of religious belief and practice.

Youth in the United States have a far poorer church attendance record than do their elders, but they are not so anti-church nor anti-religion as is sometimes believed. Nor do they raise any basic theological arguments. For them, God is very much alive.

Yet, a significant number of youth fault the nation's churches and church members in one basic respect—"failing to meet the daily needs of people." What young people today are seeking, I believe, is not "social protest" (official statements from church leaders on society's ills) so much as they are seeking "social action." Youth sometimes tend to think of organized religion as a "closed club" of older, affluent people who work on committees, but don't get involved in the really tough, unheralded but rewarding sacrificial person-to-person kind of work needed—helping the sick, the poor, the elderly—with their time and energy and prayers, not just their money.

Young people today have been misnamed the "self-centered generation." In fact, they have a strongly-developed sense of service to society with many hoping to enter the "helping professions," including social work. They would, therefore, likely look unfavorably upon one recent estimate that American churches spend 80 percent of their revenues for internal purposes, leaving 20 percent for the poor and the oppressed.

One of the tasks of religious leaders is to link the apparent will to believe among young people with their interest in helping others. Some might maintain that such a link would result in merely a dry "faith-in-works" kind of service rather than service energized by a living, vital and active faith. What is needed, they would argue, are *spiritual counseling* programs—to encourage *inner* renewal for *social* renewal. In this regard, leaders of local churches should determine whether their youth ministers are merely duplicating the efforts of recreational personnel or whether they are encouraging prayer and service.

In view of the number of youth today who are caught up in the meditation movement, it clearly behooves religious leaders to provide programs for spiritual guidance. But will concentration on the inner life cause one to retreat into himself and neglect his duties to his neighbor? Many religious authorities would insist the opposite occurs—that the natural consequence of an intense inner life is an overflow of love manifested in action.

ANOTHER VIEW ON "REVIVAL" [4]

The results of the Gallup Poll are utterly misleading.
For many years I have given questionnaires to my students
in an upper-class undergraduate course in philosophy of
religion. These questionnaires are always handed out during
the first meeting of the class and returned at the end of the
hour. The students need not sign the questionnaires, and
virtually none of them do; but they always seem to find the
exercise interesting and educational. Over the years there
have been many unbelievers who pray often and many Christians who take their religion very seriously but never pray.
What is more startling, however, is their ignorance of the
Bible.

In the fall of 1976 the course was offered again after a
lapse of eight years and, of more than two dozen Princeton
students, only one was able to "name five of the Hebrew
prophets." A few others put down five names. Of the students who said that they did "consider the Bible the revealed
word of God," one could not name a single prophet;
another put down Samuel, David, and Job; yet another
could name only one prophet. The students were also asked
to indicate whether they knew the Old Testament—and
then also the New Testament—thoroughly, fairly well or
very little. . . .

Religious beliefs are not really pervasive in the United
States. Most Americans do not know what exactly they believe, never having given much thought to the matter. When
suddenly asked about what they believe, they give responses
that go back to the time when they last talked about such
questions, many years ago. People who say that they believe
in the literal interpretation of the Bible do not know, in
most cases, what is in the Bible and would be rather surprised if anyone told them. The students in my course, who
are surely better educated than most people, had to read

[4] From "Criticizing Religious Beliefs," by Walter Kaufmann, professor of
philosophy, Princeton University. *Humanist.* 37:42–3. Mr./Ap. '77. This article first
appeared in *The Humanist* March/April 1977 and is reprinted by permission.

several books of the Old and New Testaments, completely, and discovered all sorts of things they had never known.

People may say that they believe in immortality and yet be hard put to say whether they believe that one goes to heaven or hell right after death, or whether one is consigned to one or the other only at the Last Judgment. To most people who claim to believe in immortality, it has never even occurred that there is this difference. Belief in heaven is far more popular than belief in hell, and few of those who claim to believe in hell consider the prospect that they might possibly go there. Hell is strictly for others.

Even more theologians equivocate about hell, leaving unclear whether they believe in it, or whether they believe that anybody is actually in hell, or for what precisely people are damned eternally; and yet these same people preach, talk, and write about the nature of God and his relation to man. To bring up the subject of hell is widely considered indelicate, although it would be hard to think of a more important question than whether some, or even more, human beings are headed for eternal torture. What reigns supreme in religious matters is thoughtlessness.

Whose failure is this? First of all, my experience with undergraduates over the last thirty years suggests that in the Sunday schools they attended they learned nothing about religions other than their own and next to nothing about their own. The educational failure of most Sunday schools seems total.

Second, most of our colleges, including the most prestigious, give undergraduate and graduate degrees to people who are religiously illiterate. Students are made to read reams of material that have no lasting value; but they never read the Bible or the [Buddhist] Dhammapada, the [Chinese] Tao Teh Ching or the [Hindu] Bhagavadgita.

To single out "the critics of traditional religions" for failing to make their position better known makes little sense. If a man publishes several books that deal critically with religion and reaches a wide audience, he should not ascribe the thoughtlessness of so many of his fellowmen to his own failure to reach more readers. Nor would it be gracious for him to recite a long litany about people who applauded this or that book privately but failed to champion it publicly. But it needs to be said that the third great failure is not that of the critics of traditional religion who have taken a public stand, but rather that of the hundreds who have not spoken out.

That the beliefs to which so many people pay lip service respond to some deep needs is like saying that the fact that so many men wear neckties points to a deep need. In both cases we are confronted by unthinking conformism. Does it "defy easy treatment"? Making people more thoughtful is not enough as long as there are real or imagined penalties for not conforming. In the 1950s there were penalties in both cases; in the late 1970s there is more freedom in both cases. In the fifties politicians had to invoke God frequently; in the seventies there was much apprehension about a presidential candidate because he actually seemed to be serious about God. . . .

Finally, I was asked, "Most important, what ought skeptics and humanists to do, if anything? Do we need a new strategy . . . ?" I am not an organization man and have gone it alone for a long time. But I should certainly welcome more support. I do not see the picture . . . as a battle between the children of light and the children of darkness. There are many faults greater than a thoughtless belief in immortality or God—for example, disbelief coupled with the lack of the courage to defend it publicly.

It is puerile to feel enraged by what one takes to be false or confused beliefs. There are worse enemies. And a man can believe that he has been "born again" and do a lot of good. But as a teacher of philosophy or any number of other subjects, one has the duty to teach one's students to think more conscientiously; and as a writer—depending, of course, on the kind of writing one does—one may have the same duty toward one's readers. For a long time, however, even those who felt this obligation have leaned over backwards not to deal too critically with truly vital questions.

It was considered a virtue—indeed a necessary condition of respectability—to think painstakingly only about academic questions.

In the late sixties it became fashionable to deal with some substantive questions—but not very painstakingly. The social conscience prevailed over the intellectual conscience. I wish more intellectuals, scholars, teachers, and writers would deal critically with the most important questions of faith, morals, and politics. . . . Students like those described above are not in any way pernicious. What is bad is that even the best universities in a wealthy country that prides itself on its colleges should provide such a poor education. What is bad is that, in a democracy in which there is so much freedom to speak, write, and learn, most people are so thoughtless. Religious beliefs need to be considered in this larger perspective.

A "LOSS OF SPIRIT" [5]

It is quite possible to argue that the notion of a crisis in American religion is an invention of intellectuals. Recent surveys show that some 40 percent of the population is in church every week; religious books make up one of the most expansive sectors of the publishing industry; and college students continue to crowd religion courses.

The notion of crisis, however, cannot be dismissed that easily. Institutions may go on working in an externally successful way, but if the spirit has gone out of them, the prognosis for the future is not good. Regrettably, there are grounds for believing that the spirit has gone out of American religious institutions. This loss of spirit has serious implications for the larger society.

From the beginnings of American society there has been a peculiar relation between religion as embodied in the churches and the "creed" of the democratic polity—what has come to be called the civil religion of America. "True

[5] From "Battered Pillars of the American System: Religion," by Peter Berger, professor of sociology, Rutgers University. *Fortune.* 91:134–5 +. Ap. '75. Reprinted by permission from *Fortune* magazine, © 1975 Time Inc.

religion," said George Washington, "affords government its surest support." And over the years, numerous observers of the American scene have maintained that the political health of the society is nurtured by the vitality of the churches. It should not be surprising, then, that today there appear to be linkages between the spiritual crisis in the churches and the condition of the overall System.

In recent decades, religion in America has been characterized by an accelerating accommodation to nonreligious culture. The effects of this secularization of the churches have been most obviously devastating in mainstream Protestantism. Many of its thinkers and church leaders responded to the deepening secularity of the society by celebrating it. The huge success of Harvey Cox's *The Secular City*, published in 1965, did not initiate the celebration (indeed, the book was singularly unoriginal), but did ratify and broadcast it.

The situation came to be redefined in an interesting way. Not only was secularism no longer to be seen as the enemy of the churches: in a total reversal of tradition, accommodation to secular culture was to be the true realization of the churches' faith. The comic, and indeed masochistic, aspects of this redefinition were not very widely perceived; but if ever there was an ideology of rape produced by the rapee, this was it. An especially grotesque manifestation of this attitude came along about a year after Cox's book, in the media-promoted "death of God theology"—the ultimate fulfillment of any religion editor's prayer for a good man-bites-dog story.

Those who followed Cox's lead had learned to take their cues from a rather small elite of fashionable intellectuals, who, supposedly, knew where things were at. In the late Sixties, many churchmen jumped on every bandwagon announced as important by intellectual fashion. By and large, these bandwagons were either politically left or countercultural in character.

Needless to say, this did not mean that most members of the mainstream Protestant denominations joined the political left or the counterculture. What did happen was that there developed a widening gap between the leadership and the man in the pew, who often was not prepared to follow the ecclesiastical avant-garde in either its theological or its politico-cultural extravaganzas. The outcome of this tension between leaders and members was not so much a rebellion as a sour hangover following the turmoil of the late Sixties—a whimper rather than a bang. There have been of late some signs that out of this misadventure may come a new seriousness about the theological content of mainstream Protestantism, but the costs of the years of frantic accommodationism will be felt for a long time.

Evangelical Protestantism

Evangelical Protestantism survived this period not only with little if any damage to its religious substance but also with a new aggressive spirit. It is this sector of the Protestant community that has been growing most vigorously. But the intactness of evangelical Protestantism has been greatly helped by a relative isolation from the dynamics of the national culture. The isolation was partly self-imposed and partly the result of geographical or class boundaries—evangelical Protestantism had achieved little penetration in the urbanized areas of the country or in the upper-middle class. The new aggressiveness of these denominations, expressed both in evangelism beyond the traditional clienteles and in a new social activism, will, rather paradoxically, bring them into much closer contact with the forces of secularism. It remains to be seen how well the "old-time religion" will bear up under this new intimacy with the national culture.

Roman Catholicism

Until Vatican II, the Roman Catholic community in this country was in a situation of cultural isolation not greatly dissimilar from that of evangelical Protestantism. The rapid tumbling of the walls since then has been all the more remarkable. This process too has a comic aspect. The progressive reformers believed that their actions would make the church a more vital force in the society. Instead, these actions have plunged the church into its most severe crisis of credibility in recent history.

Every theological, cultural, and political folly of the Protestant avant-garde was enthusiastically embraced by its Catholic counterparts, who jumped on bandwagons with all the fervor of teenagers newly released from the strict discipline of school—those tight-lipped teaching nuns finally got their comeuppance. In all this excitement it took some time for the reformers to notice that many Catholics were more dismayed than inspired by the new look in their parishes. If the roof has not been blown off thus far, the main reason is probably the instinctive conservatism of the church authorities, both in Rome and in the American episcopate. Be this as it may, the spiritual hangover has today become ecumenical in scope.

Judaism

It has also become interfaith. Jews have been no more immune to the accommodationist wave than Christians, but with an additional paradoxical twist: At the precise moment when, for reasons that have little to do with religion, there is a new sense of a need for Jewish identity and solidarity, the erosion of religious substance makes the fulfillment of this need acutely difficult.

In sum, the most significant development in the area of denominational religion has been a monumental failure of nerve. From the viewpoint of religious faith, this would have been a sorry development under any circumstances. In the circumstances of contemporary America, the development has been both ironic and devastating, for the secular culture to which the churches were called to accommodate themselves has itself been going through a profound failure of nerve. The schoolboys, having hopped on the bandwagon, are still exclaiming that they have at last been liberated—while the bandwagon is rapidly falling apart beneath them. The secular city, it turns out, was made of cardboard. And whatever glue held the construction together was derived from just those old materials that had been so joyfully cast aside.

According to the conventional wisdom of liberal commentators, the crisis of self-confidence in American culture can be traced to the racial conflict, the war in Indochina, and Watergate. There can be no doubt that these events contributed materially, but it should give pause that other nations, not burdened with these particular experiences, have been going through very similar crises.

Very likely there are deeper causes, rooted in the underlying structure of advanced modern societies, with the aforementioned events serving as triggers or as aggravating factors in the case of the U.S. Whatever may be the final historical explanation of all this, it is clear that the American civil religion, the political "creed" of the society, has suffered considerable damage during these years.

II. PROTESTANT DIVERSITY

EDITOR'S INTRODUCTION

As it has been since the founding of the Republic, Protestantism is the religious faith of the largest number of Americans. The first article in this section, from *Senior Scholastic*, provides background information on the wide variety of beliefs and practices found in the many churches of the Protestant faith.

The four selections that follow deal with a significant theological controversy of recent years, in which contrasting views are strongly expressed as to religion's proper response to conditions of today's world. This controversy takes the form of the Appeal for Theological Affirmation (the Hartford Affirmation)—which called for a retreat from modern Christianity's increasing emphasis on social issues—and the Boston Affirmations—which defended the idea of social consciousness. In each case, the pronouncements were created by diverse groups of clergymen, the majority of them Protestant.

Involving a far wider range of practicing Protestants is the current surge of evangelicalism. This is defined as "the religion you get when you 'get' religion. . . . All evangelicals are united by a subjective experience of personal salvation, which they describe as being 'born again,' converted or regenerated." This experience is detailed, first by David F. Wells and John D. Woodbridge—who describe the historical background of evangelicalism—and then in a selection from *Newsweek* (from which the preceding quotation is excerpted).

In the next two articles, New York *Times* reporter Kenneth A. Briggs writes on the beliefs and attitudes of "charismatic Christians," and *Village Voice* senior editor Robert Christgau examines the Southern Baptist faith of

the most celebrated "born again" individual, President
Jimmy Carter.

The final selection is by Edward L. Ericson, a leader of
the Society for Ethical Culture, a group that emphasizes
ethical beliefs and moral practices rather than divine guidance. Ericson comments here on the evangelical movement
from a secular humanist standpoint.

THE MANY HOUSES OF PROTESTANTISM [1]

Incense lamps swing solemnly on silent chains. Smoke
curls slowly through the pastel shafts of light penetrating
the stained glass windows. A solemn acolyte approaches
the altar carrying a huge, jewel-studded cross. Two other
boy walk at his sides, each holding a three-foot-high golden
candle. The priest, resplendent in intricately embroidered
robes, raises a golden chalice and consecrates the dark wine
within it. A choir chants softly.

A medieval service in a venerable English abbey? No.
It is 1977, and we are witnessing a high mass in an Episcopal
cathedral.

The scene shifts. Business-suited evangelist Billy Graham
addresses 50,000 worshippers in a baseball stadium hired
for the occasion. Six hundred giant billboards announced
his coming. Special sound and lighting effects amplify God's
message. The Reverend warns of a "divine computer" that
compiles everyone's record of sins with terrifying efficiency.
Each of us, he stresses, must find God before the final print-
out.

The scene shifts again. We are in the Amish country
of Pennsylvania. Men in somber black suits and broad-
brimmed hats, women in old-fashioned bonnets and long
black dresses, are leaving their neat farms for the all-day
Sabbath service. They ride in horse-drawn buggies. The

[1] From "Protestantism—World Religions: Part 6." *Senior Scholastic.* 109:22–
4+. Ap. 7, '77. Reprinted by permission from *Senior Scholastic,* © 1977 by
Scholastic Magazines Inc.

Bible doesn't mention cars or telephones or trains or planes, so the Amish do without them.

Now we are in a Quaker meeting-house. There are no stained glass windows. There is no altar, no organ, no steeple, no ordained minister. The Friends (as the Quakers call themselves) meet in silent meditation and wait for a spiritual message to move one of them to speak. If no one gets a message during the worship hour, everyone will get up and go home. Not a word will have been spoken.

In an Appalachian log church or Indiana tent meeting, hands clap and feet stomp to the rhythms of tambourines and electric guitars. Here and there, someone falls to the ground in a trance—"saved" by coming to Jesus Crist.

In thousands of churches, millions of worshippers spend an hour each Sunday in quiet prayer, listening to the message of their minister, and reading the words of the Bible.

The Bond of Protest

What common bond holds this diverse collection of worshippers together? It is a history of religious protest—all are Protestants. "In my father's house there are many rooms," said Jesus. The diversity of Protestant sects seems to support his words. . . .

Although they often differed in other ways, early Protestants all rejected the authority of the Roman Catholic Pope. This distinguished them from Catholics. But soon, some Protestants began to feel that their own established Protestant sects were getting away from what they considered the true Christian principles. Some of these people started new groups—not with the intention of adding a new dimension to Christianity, but aiming to return it to the old-time religion they felt others had corrupted.

The Protestant branch of the Christian family tree keeps growing new shoots. Today, there are about 80 separate Protestant groups in the U.S. alone—Baptists, Lutherans, Episcopalians, Methodists, Presbyterians, Seventh Day Adventists, Jehovah's Witnesses, Quakers, Christian Scientists,

and more. Many of these divide themselves even further—
there are, for instance, 22 branches of the Baptist faith. All
together, about half of all American Christians are Protestants. But because of their tendency to separate, the largest
religious domination in the U.S.—by far—is Roman Catholicism.

The range of Protestant beliefs is enormous, as shown
in a recent survey undertaken by the University of California. Some examples: 97% of Southern Baptists polled
said that it is "absolutely necessary" to believe in Jesus
Christ in order to be saved; only 38% of Congregationalists
polled agreed. Only 32% of Episcopalians believe that every
word of the Bible is *literally* true; 80% of Missouri Synod
Lutherans insist it is. Only 22% of Congregationalists think
there is a real, live devil; nearly every Southern Baptist—
99%—believe the devil exists.

Episcopalians believe, along with Roman Catholics, that
there are seven sacraments at the heart of Christian worship.
But most Protestants consider ony two sacraments—baptism
and holy communion—divinely ordained. Some Protestant
faiths dispense with sacraments altogether. Differences over
the need for church attendance, over social activism, over the
conditions of salvation also abound among Protestants.

There is, however, at least one thing they all agree on—
they don't believe that the Pope has the authority to interpret God's word. Instead, Protestants go directly to the
Bible. Most Protestants believe that anyone can understand
by himself what the Bible says and what it means—the
"priesthood of all believers," it is sometimes called. This
does not mean that all who read the Bible agree on what
the words mean. There are many different interpretations,
as many as there are Christian faiths.

The Shattering of Christendom

There was only one church in Medieval Western Europe
—the Roman Catholic Church, headed by the Pope in
Rome. The Church's authority, political as well as theological, was nearly complete. Anyone who challenged the

Church was branded a heretic, and unrepentant heretics could be burned at the stake.

By the end of the 15th century, Europe was changing dramatically. Countries of northern Europe were growing more powerful. Kings and emperors—far from Rome and the Pope's influence—resented the Church's power. The Renaissance spread new ideas. Industry grew. Cities sprang up, establishing a new middle class which began to resent the Church's authority. And corruption had infected the Church itself.

It was during this time of upheaval that a young German monk—Martin Luther—began questioning some of the basic teachings of the Church. Luther taught theology at the University of Wittenberg. He was a devout Catholic. But he was plagued by personal doubts and suffered over the state of his eternal soul. How, he asked himself, does a human please God?

Seeking Inner Peace

The Church emphasized that in order for eternal salvation man had to (1) have faith, and (2) do good works—that is, pray, fast, give alms, and follow all Church teachings. Luther did all these things; he even whipped himself in penitence for his sins. But he didn't *feel* the peace that he knew should come when he would truly be saved.

Luther slowly reached the conclusion that he couldn't save himself from eternal damnation. Only God could save him. As a Christian, Luther believed that Christ had died to save mankind from its own sins. To be saved, therefore, a Christian must recognize Christ as the savior. That belief was all that was necessary.

God gave Christ to the world as an example, Luther reasoned. By resurrecting Jesus, God showed the world that He was willing to save mankind. A human being can accept that salvation by acknowledging Christ as the savior. Someone who refuses to accept Christ will be damned forever. No number of good works, no amount of fasting or praying can save him from the fires of hell. Salvation, Luther concluded, is a gift that God gives to those who truly accept Christ.

Besides disputing Church doctrine, Luther was angered by the corruption he saw growing up within the Church. He was especially incensed by the sale of indulgences—a sort of "ticket to heaven" being sold by some emissaries of the Pope as a way of raising money. These indulgences, sold to the faithful, were supposed to help get them or departed relatives to heaven faster.

Angered by these and other practices which he felt were corrupting the true Christian faith, Luther, in 1517, struck the blow that shattered Christendom. He nailed his Ninety-five Theses, an attack against the practice of selling indulgences, to the door of Wittenberg cathedral.

Political Consequences

Although Luther had not intended to leave the Church (he wanted reforms), the argument between him and the Pope escalated to the point where Luther was declared a heretic and excommunicated (1521). In earlier times, this would undoubtedly have meant death. But Luther found some powerful protectors among the ruling princes of the many small German states.

By backing Luther, these rulers were freed from paying the heavy taxes demanded by the Catholic Church. This—plus Luther's personal appeal—caused many to convert to Lutheranism. And in those days, when a ruler converted, the people under his rule had to convert. In this way the Reformation, as it is called by Protestants—or the Protestant Revolution as it has been called by Catholics—had important political as well as theological consequences.

The most famous reformer after Luther was John Calvin, whose strict teachings were later followed by the Puritan settlers of the New World. Calvin went a step further than Luther in his break with Catholic doctrine. He said that accepting Christ will not save you, nor will good behavior. Calvin said that God saves only those He chooses to save. If you're not one of the "chosen," there's nothing you can do to save yourself. How do you know if you're one of the chosen? You don't—only God does. But Calvin believed that those whom God had chosen would lead a virtuous life on Earth.

Luther and Calvin and others shook the Catholic Church to its foundations, attacking its authority and teachings. Church leaders struck back. They organized a Counter-Reformation, demanding certain reforms from within. The new Society of Jesus (whose members are called Jesuits) formed to spread the Catholic message and win back some of the converts to Catholicism. The Jesuits did especially well in Eastern Europe.

The contest for converts became a bloody one. The vicious Thirty Years' War (1618–1648), for example, wiped out half the German population. Eventually, however, both Catholics and Protestants turned to more peaceful methods of winning converts. And today, happily, Catholics and Protestants generally live peacefully together. (Northern Ireland is a tragic exception, but there the differences are based on economics as much as—if not more than—religion.)

Coming Together?

New Protestant churches continued to form even to this day. But much like the Vatican II spirit of fellowship, the more common tendency among Protestants today is to reach out to one another and even to regroup into larger churches. In 1939, for example, Methodist churches of the North and South repaired a division that had existed since the Civil War. In 1957 the United Church of Christ was formed from the Congregational, Evangelical, and Reformed groups. Many smaller Lutheran churches in the U.S. have combined in the past 20 years.

Furthermore, the two main branches of Christianity in America—Protestantism and Roman Catholicism—have come closer together, at least as far as recognizing each other as legitimate expressions of Christian belief.

THE NEW HERETICS [2]

When eighteen prominent theologians met in Hartford, Conn., last winter to deal with some "false" notions in modern Christianity, they anticipated a lukewarm response from their churchly brethren. But the "Appeal for Theological Affirmation" that they issued immediately touched a raw nerve among the country's clergy. "We are enormously surprised by the thunderous effect it has had," says Lutheran Rev. Richard Neuhaus, an author of the document and editor of the religious journal *Worldview*. "It has become a major point of reference."

It has also become a major source of theological controversy. Concerned that the increasing emphasis on social action had obscured the primary mission of Christianity, the Hartford theologians called for a return to a direct, transcendent relationship with God. The signers of the appeal, representing nearly every major denomination, attacked the church's "surrender to secularism" and to other worldly "diseases" from the activist 1960s. "People were equating [the] Esalen [Institute, a California-based consciousness-raising group] with theology, a marijuana high with a religious experience and calling masturbation a sacrament," says co-author Peter Berger, a Lutheran sociologist. "There was a readiness for a sobering word." [See Professor Berger's article "A Loss of Spirit," in Section I, above.]

Hundreds of letters supporting the Hartford back-to-basics approach poured in to the signers—some from clergy whose dwindling congregations bore out Berger's belief that the church's "capitulation to the culture" was alienating Christian congregants. At the same time, dozens of theologians and academics attacked the appeal for being trendy and arrogant. . . .

Among the thirteen "heresies" repudiated by the Hartford group and their supporters is the belief that contempo-

[2] Excerpts from article by Susan Cheever Cowley and Laurie Lisle. *Newsweek.* 86:64. S. 29, 75. Copyright 1975 by Newsweek, Inc. All rights reserved. Reprinted by permission.

rary thought is superior to traditional answers, and that Jesus can only be understood in terms of modern man. Such themes as "all religions are equally valid," and that "to realize one's potential . . . is the whole meaning of salvation" are blasphemous, says Neuhaus. "Religion had become a silly imitation of what was happening in the marketplace. Christianity lost its nerve to challenge the culture." The appeal even cuts across sociopolitical lines. According to the Hartford definition, the Episcopal Rev. William Wendt of Washington, D.C., who has led the fight for women's ordination, and Harvard theologian Harvey Cox (*The Secular City*) are as guilty of worldliness as preacher Norman Vincent Peale and the evangelical Reverend Ike. This across-the-board indictment, says Neuhaus, took a "lot of *chutzpa* [nerve]—but then anything worth doing is worth doing pretentiously."

Angry dissent has erupted on all sides. Church historian Martin Marty shrugged off the heresies as themes that most active Christians had already repudiated. Furthermore, he charged, the Hartford signers were as guilty as those attacked. "Nothing is more 'with it' and 'relevant' in 1975," he said, "than attacking the idea of being 'with it' and 'relevant'.". . . And Canadian Catholic priest Gregory Baum objected to the tone and the timing of the appeal, suggesting that a call for amnesty for draft evaders would have been appropriate.

The predominantly white male composition of the Hartford group has added to the controversy. Harvey Cox replied to the appeal with a list of what he considers more important heresies; including the beliefs that the theology of the white Western world is the mainstream and that women should be excluded from equality in the church. . . .

Transcendence

But Neuhaus, a former antiwar activist who worked with the Rev. Martin Luther King Jr., believes that only after the churches are "straightened out" will they have "the nerve to go about making social changes." And Peter Berger, a Rutgers professor, believes that the new emphasis on transcendence may even recapture Christians who have turned to drugs, sects and pseudopsychology looking for an experience their church failed to offer. Whether or not it has that impact, at the very least the Hartford appeal is the first significant questioning of the church's increasing social and political involvement.

THE BOSTON AFFIRMATIONS [3]

In the 1960s mainstream Protestants in America were swept up in such social crusades as civil rights and opposition to the Vietnam war. Since then, however, something of a reaction has set in. Denominations have trimmed their social sails, and many activist preachers have turned inward, emphasizing personal psychological needs.

Theologians too have shifted ground. Some have feared that the swing toward social involvement undercut belief in a God who ultimately transcends the affairs of this world. A year ago, a group of them met in Hartford, Conn., and issued a dramatic "Appeal for Theological Affirmation" [see the preceding and following articles]. The Hartford group—mostly Protestant but with a number of Roman Catholics and Eastern Orthodox joining in the effort—hurled anathemas against 13 "false and debilitating" themes, including the belief that "the struggle for a better humanity will bring about the Kingdom of God."

That aroused the liberals, who were already on the defensive and felt that the Hartford appeal strengthened a dangerous trend. Last week the latest in a series of responses to Hartford was unleashed by a 21-member task force of the Boston Industrial Mission. (Cambridge-based, the B.I.M. was set up by Protestant churches in 1965 to raise issues of ethics and social justice among the Boston area's business, technological and industrial professionals.) It is a counter-

[3] From "Counterattack." *Time.* 107:50. Ja. 19, '76. Reprinted by permission from *Time,* the Weekly Newsmagazine; Copyright Time Inc. 1976.

attack called "The Boston Affirmations" and it constitutes a theological rallying cry against any retreat from social action. [For text see below in this section.]

Insisting that the Social Gospel is not dead, the Boston group is enthusiastic about the struggle by the world's poor for a better material life, the drive for "ethnic dignity," women's campaign against "sexist subordination" in church and society, and efforts to foster a love for cities as "centers of civility, culture and human interdependence."

If the last sounds like an echo of the liberal Protestant bible of the mid-1960s, *The Secular City*, it is no coincidence. The best-known member of the Boston group is that book's author, Harvey Cox of Harvard Divinity School, who joined the other signers in the scruffy B.I.M. office to celebrate the "Affirmations" with a liturgy and a lunch of jug Burgundy and ham-and-cheese sandwiches. Besides Cox, the task force included black theologian Preston Williams of Harvard, a Chicago theologian from California, a local pastor laden with preliminary documents for the World Council of Churches assembly, and social ethicist Max Stackhouse of Andover Newton Theological School, who edited the various drafts of the pronouncement.

Fall and Exodus

Despite the continuing argument, there is some convergence between heavenly Hartford and worldly Boston. The Hartford theologians, no social dropouts, insist that emphasis on God's "transcendence" and traditional faith is not only compatible with social action but strengthens it. The Bostonians profess that God "brings into being all resources, all life" and, on that basis, insist that Christians have a responsibility to tackle social ills. The argument proceeds through eight sections, bearing traditional titles ("Creation," "Fall" and "Exodus").

The Boston statement ends on a note of eloquence. When Hartford-style "spiritual blindness" wins out, it says, "the world as God's creation is abandoned, sin rules, liberation is frustrated, covenant is broken, prophecy is stilled, wisdom is betrayed, suffering love is transformed into triviality."

TEXT OF THE HARTFORD APPEAL [4]

The renewal of Christian witness and mission requires constant examination of the assumptions shaping the Church's life. Today an apparent loss of a sense of the transcendent is undermining the Church's ability to address with clarity and courage the urgent tasks to which God calls it in the world. This loss is manifest in a number of pervasive themes. Many are superficially attractive, but upon closer examination we find these themes false and debilitating to the Church's life and work. Among such themes are:

> *Theme 1: Modern thought is superior to all past forms of understanding reality, and is therefore normative for Christian faith and life.*

In repudiating this theme we are protesting the captivity to the prevailing thought structures not only of the twentieth century but of any historical period. We favor using any helpful means of understanding, ancient or modern, and insist that the Christian proclamation must be related to the idiom of the culture. At the same time, we affirm the need for Christian thought to confront and be confronted by other worldviews, all of which are necessarily provisional.

> *Theme 2: Religious statements are totally independent of reasonable discourse.*

The capitulation to the alleged primacy of modern thought takes two forms: one is the subordination of religious statements to the canons of scientific rationality; the other, equating reason with scientific rationality, would remove religious statements from the realm of reasonable discourse altogether. A religion of pure subjectivity and non-rationality results in treating faith statements as being,

---

[4] "An Appeal for Theological Affirmation." In *Worldview Symposium on the Hartford Appeal.* Council on Religion and International Affairs. 170 E. 64th St. New York 10021. '75. p 3–4.

at best, statements about the believer. We repudiate both forms of capitulation.

Theme 3: Religious language refers to human experience and nothing else, God being humanity's noblest creation.

Religion is also a set of symbols and even of human projections. We repudiate the assumption that it is nothing but that. What is here at stake is nothing less than the reality of God: *We did not invent God; God invented us.*

Theme 4: Jesus can only be understood in terms of contemporary models of humanity.

This theme suggests a reversal of "the imitation of Christ"; that is, the image of Jesus is made to reflect cultural and countercultural notions of human excellence. We do not deny that all aspects of humanity are illumined by Jesus. Indeed, it is necessary to the universality of the Christ that he be perceived in relation to the particularities of the believers' world. We do repudiate the captivity to such metaphors, which are necessarily inadequate, relative, transitory, and frequently idolatrous. Jesus, together with the Scriptures and the whole of the Christian tradition, cannot arbitrarily be interpreted without reference to the history of which they are part. The danger is in the attempt to exploit the tradition without taking the tradition seriously.

Theme 5: All religions are equally valid; the choice among them is not a matter of conviction about truth but only of personal preference or lifestyle.

We affirm our common humanity. We affirm the importance of exploring and confronting all manifestations of the religious quest and of learning from the riches of other religions. But we repudiate this theme because it flattens diversities and ignores contradictions. In doing so, it not only obscures the meaning of Christian faith, but also fails to respect the integrity of other faiths. Truth matters; therefore differences among religions are deeply significant.

Theme 6: To realize one's potential and to be true to oneself is the whole meaning of salvation.

Salvation contains a promise of human fulfillment, but to identify salvation with human fulfillment can trivialize the promise. We affirm that salvation cannot be found apart from God.

Theme 7: Since what is human is good, evil can adequately be understood as failure to realize potential.

This theme invites false understanding of the ambivalence of human existence and underestimates the pervasiveness of sin. Paradoxically, by minimizing the enormity of evil, it undermines serious and sustained attacks on particular social or individual evils.

Theme 8: The sole purpose of worship is to promote individual self-realization and human community.

Worship promotes individual and communal values, but it is above all a response to the reality of God and arises out of the fundamental need and desire to know, love, and adore God. We worship God because God is to be worshiped.

Theme 9: Institutions and historical traditions are oppressive and inimical to our being truly human; liberation from them is required for authentic existence and authentic religion.

Institutions and traditions are often oppressive. For this reason they must be subjected to relentless criticism. But human community inescapably requires institutions and traditions. Without them life would degenerate into chaos and new forms of bondage. The modern pursuit of liberation from all social and historical restraints is finally dehumanizing.

Theme 10: The world must set the agenda for the Church. Social, political, and economic programs to improve the quality of life are ultimately normative for the Church's mission in the world.

This theme cuts across the political and ideological spectrum. Its form remains the same, no matter whether the content is defined as upholding the values of the American way of life, promoting socialism, or raising human consciousness. The Church must denounce oppressors, help liberate the oppressed, and seek to heal human misery. Sometimes the Church's mission coincides with the world's programs. But the norms for the Church's activity derive from its own perception of God's will for the world.

Theme 11: An emphasis on God's transcendence is at least a hindrance to, and perhaps incompatible with, Christian social concern and action.

This supposition leads some to denigrate God's transcendence. Others, holding to a false transcendence, withdraw into religious privatism or individualism and neglect the personal and communal responsibility of Christians for the earthly city. From a biblical perspective, it is precisely because of confidence in God's reign over all aspects of life that Christians must participate fully in the struggle against oppressive and dehumanizing structures and their manifestations in racism, war, and economic exploitation.

Theme 12: The struggle for a better humanity will bring about the Kingdom of God.

The struggle for a better humanity is essential to Christian faith and can be informed and inspired by the biblical promise of the Kingdom of God. But imperfect human beings cannot create a perfect society. The Kingdom of God surpasses any conceivable utopia. God has his own designs which confront ours, surprising us with judgment and redemption.

Theme 13: The question of hope beyond death is irrelevant or at best marginal to the Christian understanding of human fulfillment.

This is the final capitulation to modern thought. If death is the last word, then Christianity has nothing to say to the final questions of life. We believe that God raised Jesus from the dead and are ". . . convinced that there is nothing in death or life, in the realm of spirits or superhuman powers, in the world as it is or in the world as it shall be, in the forces of the universe, in heights or depths—nothing in all creation that can separate us from the love of God in Christ Jesus our Lord" (Romans 8:38 f.).

TEXT OF THE BOSTON AFFIRMATIONS [5]

The living God is active in current struggles to bring a Reign of Justice, Righteousness, Love and Peace. The Judeo-Christian traditions are pertinent to the dilemmas of our world. All believers are called to preach the good news to the poor, to proclaim release to the captives and recovery of sight to the blind, to set at liberty those who are oppressed and to proclaim the acceptable year of the Lord. Yet we are concerned about what we discern to be present trends in our churches, in religious thought and in our society. We see struggles in every arena of human life, but in too many parts of the church and theology we find retreat from these struggles. Still, we are not without hope nor warrants for our hope. Hopeful participation in these struggles is at once action in faith, the primary occasion for personal spiritual growth, the development of viable structures for the common life, and the vocation of the people of God. To sustain such participation we have searched the past and the present to find the signs of God's future and of ours. Thus, we make the following Affirmations:

Creation: God brings into being all resources, all life, all genuine meanings. Humanity is of one source and is not ultimately governed by nature or history, by the fabric of societies or the depths of the self, by knowledge or belief. God's triune activity sustains creative order, evokes personal identity, and is embodied in the dynamic movements of human history in an ever more inclusive community of persons responsibly engaged in all aspects of the ecosphere, history and thought.

Fall: Humanity is estranged from the source of life. We try to ignore or transcend the source and end of life. Or we

[5] From "The Boston Affirmations." *Christianity and Crisis.* 36:23–7. F. 16, '76. Reprinted by permission of the study group that produced the statement.

try to place God in a transcendent realm divorced from life. Thereby we give license to domination, indulgence, pretense, triviality and evasion. We endanger creative order, we destroy personal identity, and we corrupt inspirited communities. We allow tyranny, anarchy and death to dominate the gift of life.

Exodus and Covenant: God delivers from oppression and chaos. God chooses strangers, servants, and outcasts to be witnesses and to become a community of righteousness and mercy. Beyond domination and conflict God hears the cry of the oppressed and works vindication for all. God forms "nobodies" into a people of "somebodies," and makes known the laws of life. The liberation experience calls forth celebrative response, demands responsibility in community, and opens people and nations for a common global history.

Prophecy: In compassion God speaks to the human community through prophets. Those who authentically represent God have interpreted—and will interpret—the activity of God in social history. They announce the presence of God in the midst of political and economic life; they foretell the judgment and hope that are implicit in the loyalties and practices of the common life; and they set forth the vision of convenantal renewal.

Wisdom: The cultural insights and memories of many people and ages illuminate the human condition. The experience and lore of all cultures and groups bear within them values that are of wider meaning. Racism, genocide, imperialism, sexism are thus contrary to God's purposes and impoverish us all. Yet all wisdom must also be tested for its capacity to reveal the human dependence on the source of life, to grasp the depths of sin, to liberate, to evoke prophecy and to form genuine covenant.

The New Covenant: God is known to us in Jesus Christ. The source and end of life is disclosed in that suffering love which breaks the power of sin and death, which renders hope in the action of God to reconcile and transform the world, which shatters the barriers of ethnic, class, familial, national and caste restrictions. Meaning and divine activity are incarnate in history and human particularity.

Church Traditions: God calls those who trust the power of suffering love to form into communities of celebration, care and involvement. Those called together enact renewing forms of association and movement to the ends of the earth, responding by word and deed to the implications of faith for each age and for us today:

☐ The early Eastern church celebrated the dependence of humanity upon the cosmos, and of the cosmos upon God, demanding a sacramental attitude toward the whole of creation.

☐ The Formers of doctrine set forth the meanings of faith in the face of cultured despisers, exposed the frail foundations of various secularisms, and gave new directions to both the faithful and civilization.

☐ The Monastics assumed vows to exemplify life styles beyond preoccupation with gain, freedom from familial and sexual stereotyping, and disciplined lives of service.

☐ The Scholastics engaged secular culture, demanding of each generation critical and synthetic reappropriation of tradition.

☐ The Reformers preached the word of protest against religious pretense and demanded reliance upon the gifts of divine empowerment.

☐ The Sectarians nurtured the spirit that cannot be contained by priesthood, dogma, hierarchy, authoritative word or any established power, and demanded democracy, freedom, toleration and the redistribution of authority, power and wealth.

☐ And today many reach out for wider fellowships, demanding ecumenical engagements and a witness which frees and unites.

Wherever the heirs of these movements are authentic, they confess their sins, worship the power that sustains them, form a company of the committed, and struggle for justice and love against the powers and principalities of evil.

Present Witnesses: The question today is whether the heritage of this past can be sustained, preserved and extended into the future. Society as presently structured, piety as presently practiced, and the churches as presently preoccupied evoke profound doubts about the prospects. Yet we are surrounded by a cloud of witnesses who prophetically exemplify or discern the activity of God. The transforming reality of God's reign is found today:

☐ In the struggles of the poor to gain a share of the world's wealth, to become creative participants in the common economic life, and to move our world toward an economic democracy of equity and accountability.

☐ In the transforming drive for ethnic dignity against the persistent racism of human hearts and social institutions.

☐ In the endeavor by women to overcome sexist subordination in the church's ministry, in society at large, and in the images that bind our minds and bodies.

☐ In the attempts within families to overcome prideful domination and degrading passivity, and to establish genuine covenants of mutuality and joyous fidelity.

☐ In the efforts by many groups to develop for modern humanity a love for its cities as centers of civility, culture and human interdependence.

☐ In the demands of the sick and the elderly for inexpensive, accessible health care administered with concern, advised consent and sensitivity.

☐ In the voices of citizens and political leaders who demand honesty and openness, who challenge the misplaced trust of the nation in might, and who resist the temptations to make a nation and its institutions objects of religious loyalty.

☐ In the research of science when it warns of dangers to humanity and quests for those forms of technology which can sustain human well-being and preserve ecological resources.

☐ In the humanities and social sciences when the depths of human meanings are opened to inquiry and are allowed to open our horizons, especially whenever there is protest against the subordination of religion to scientific rationality or against [its] removal from realms of rational discourse.

☐ In the arts where beauty and meaning are explored, lifted up and represented in ways that call us to deeper sensibilities.

☐ In the halls of justice when righteousness is touched with mercy, when the prisoner and the wrongdoer are treated with dignity and fairness.

☐ And especially in those branches and divisions of the church where the truth is spoken in love, where transforming social commitments are nurtured and persons are brought to informed conviction, where piety is renewed and recast in concert with the heritage, and where such struggles as those here identified are seen as the action of the living God who alone is worshiped.

On these grounds, we cannot stand with those secular cynics and religious spiritualizers who see in such witnesses no theology, no eschatological urgency, and no Godly promise or judgment. In such spiritual blindness, secular or religious, the world as God's creation is abandoned, sin rules, liberation is frustrated, covenant is broken, prophecy is stilled, wisdom is betrayed, suffering love is transformed into triviality, and the church is transmuted into a club for self- or transcendental awareness. The struggle is now joined for the future of faith and the common life. We call all who believe in the living God to affirm, to sustain and to extend these witnesses.

RESURGENCE OF EVANGELICAL
PROTESTANTISM [6]

The current resurgence of evangelical Protestantism, coming as it does after an era of painful eclipse and emerg-

[6] From *The Evangelicals*, ed. by David F. Wells and John D. Woodbridge. Abingdon Press. '75. p 9-16. Copyright © 1975 by Abingdon Press. Used by permission. Dr. Wells is chairman of the department of church history and history of Christian thought at Trinity Evangelical Divinity School; Dr. Woodbridge is associate professor of church history.

ing under the high noon of secularism, constitutes a remarkable historical development. The development seems particularly notable because the demise of evangelical Protestantism, both in the popular imagination and the academic mind, had appeared so complete. Even the major role that evangelicalism had played in shaping American culture in the nineteenth century seemed generally forgotten, and progressive views of historical development assumed that once the pattern of twentieth-century evangelical decline was established it could not be substantially reversed. The fact that the movement now can no longer be regarded as simply reactionary, but is vigorously and sometimes creatively speaking to the needs of the contemporary world is a phenomenon that has already brought considerable comment and which deserves further analysis. . . .

By the middle third of the nineteenth century, evangelical Protestantism, led principally by theological conservatives, dominated American religion. It received its life impulse from the periodic revivals which coursed through the land and forced into retreat both deism and skepticism, those children of the Enlightenment. . . .

The Civil War marked a watershed in American church history. Existing ecclesiastical divisions among evangelicals over the slavery issue were dramatically reinforced by the north-south split. Christians in the north and the south were no longer quite as confident that God's blessing was upon them and their land. Moreover black evangelicals and white evangelicals went their separate ways as the country moved through the Reconstruction Era (1865–1877) and beyond into the ignominious period of "Jim Crow" legislation.

In the closing decades of the last century the fact that the evangelical heyday might be ending was signaled in many other ways, not least of all in the educational realm. Institutions of higher learning were now assaulted by a barrage of bewildering ideas of a philosophical and scientific nature. Biblical criticism, basically a German import, eroded confidence in the integrity of the biblical text. . . .

In the 1920s and 1930s . . . [the] tendency to separate from theological error and evil within society was instrumental in bringing about massive denominational disruptions. Threatened by the intrusion of Modernism into the mainline denominations, many theological conservatives (often referred to as fundamentalists) withdrew to establish their own "purer" organizations which in turn sponsored "purer" educational institutions. The enemy—proponents of evolution, Marxists, theological liberals, Catholic immigrants—was fought on all sides, and nowhere was this better exemplified than in a courtroom in Tennessee.

The Scopes Trial of 1925, ostensibly about the issue of evolution, in fact posed a question of larger import: Could a representative of conservative Christianity repulse the challenge of "modern" science? As the town of Dayton [Tennessee] awaited the answer, its streets were transformed into a festive hawker's haven with bustling crowds and reporters from the country's leading newspapers. During the proceedings, the large audience cheered, scoffed, and sat silent while the two giants did battle. William Jennings Bryan, the silver-tongued orator and three-time presidential candidate of the Democratic Party, now aging and clearly ill at ease in questions of a scientific nature, frequently was caught off balance by John Scopes' brilliant defender, Clarence Darrow. With the whole country looking on, conservative Christianity was not only repulsed, but seemingly crushed. . . .

The period from the 1930s to the 1960s, bracketed by the Depression on the one end and the Vietnam war on the other, was in many ways one of lonely consolidation. Wounds were licked, losses were counted, defenses were shored up. Thus when the liberal Federal Council of Churches seemed to be acquiring undue power, a parallel movement, the National Association of Evangelicals, was formed in 1942 to represent those more conservatively minded. William Ward Ayer, who addressed an early meeting, argued that fragmentation had cost evangelicals a voice in the nation's affairs. Ayer's assessment of the consequences

of two decades of withdrawal and division was undoubtedly
correct, but his call to unity could only be partly heeded;
Carl McIntire, whose concerns were more decidedly fundamentalistic, had already formed another organization, the
American Council of Christian Churches (1941). Common
to many evangelicals in this period was the belief that the
gospel and the "American way of life" were not only corre-
lates but almost synonyms. Coexisting with revivalistic faith
was sometimes found idolatrous patriotism; the Flag was
often draped over the Cross, and both were revered as belonging together.

In the 1950s the general "revival" in religious interest in
the nation as a whole also benefited evangelicals. A more
receptive climate was apparent. Conservative seminaries
continued to enjoy growing support, and evangelical scholarship was given a boost by the founding of Fuller Theological Seminary (1947) in Pasadena, California, and its
subsequent development. Billy Graham in his crusades was
accorded a national hearing. Campus Crusade for Christ,
founded by Bill Bright, began to recruit staff workers. Other
organizations such as Youth for Christ and Word of Life
effectively reached out to high schoolers.

For most Americans, however, this revival was as patriotic as it was religious. It often amounted to little more than
the shining and polishing of the status quo; "revival" was
virtually synonymous with the unmitigated complacency
of traditionalism. . . .

By 1958, historians spoke of the revival as being in the
past, and in one of those startling shifts of mood the Christian world found itself on the threshold of a revolutionary
era. Toward the middle 1960s it became apparent that there
was a sense of dislocation in the nation, of things being out
of harmony, of institutions adrift, of antagonism—"us"
and "them." A pervasive apprehension became apparent,
its expression oscillating between anger and helpless
docility.

Dramatic changes in accepted ways of thinking occurred.
A search for new life-styles, for different modes of belief,

and behavior, was initiated. This search blossomed into a vigorous and irreverent counterculture. Across the land there was profound social turmoil, and in the minds of many of the young, a growing distrust of the whole American system. The peace movement, the sit-ins, the civil rights marches, and the agitations all grew out of a deeply felt outrage over the kind of values that our society had not only accepted but also institutionalized. In the midst of burning cities and bombed universities, it was hoped that human dignity could be recovered, the sanctity of human life could be reasserted, both in America and in Vietnam. Corrupt and decayed as society might have been, however, it resisted all those protesters who stormed it. It did not crumble; nor did it change very much. Many of the young began to lose hope. Some became cynics. Others took refuge in the drugged sanctuary of their inner lives, still others began groping for new kinds of spirituality. Abandoning the world to its own destruction, they searched for that reality which, if unseen, would yet be more hospitable, and one whose continued existence would be more certain. In the process, some even turned away from the countercultural palliatives of drugs and promiscuous sex. By the end of the 1960s a new kind of rebel was emerging, one who was strangely quiescent, muted, preoccupied with other things, unresponsive to the manifest evils of society, passive in the face of its imminent demise.

It was during the 1960s that radical theologies blossomed and died. As a matter of fact, rank and file Christians caught in the agonies of a society trying to find itself amidst the onslaught of new and frightening problems found little help in the pronouncement that God was dead. To them, this was evidence, not of great originality, still less of truth, but merely of triviality. But it was in this period, too, that a resurgence of evangelical faith became more noticeable, providing a strange foil to the more pessimistic theologies that enjoyed their brief success.

The most flamboyant evidence of this, upon which the news media focused considerable attention, were the Jesus

People. [See "The Jesus Cult," in Section V, below.] . . .
As bizarre and newsworthy as the Jesus People were, they
represented only a small part of a far wider, far more
conventional resurgence of biblical Christianity evident
throughout the land. . . .

Whether it is proper to speak of this growth in evangelical commitment as a resurgence may be debated. It is
certainly true that in national terms evangelical Christianity
today enjoys only a fraction of the allegiance it had during
its heyday in the nineteenth century. Its influence on national priorities, the cultural outlook, education, and social
legislation remains small. It is "resurging," then, only in a
limited sense. First of all, it is proper to use this expression
when comparing the relative strengths of evangelical and
nonevangelical Protestantism; the former is growing numer-
ically and the latter is declining. Second, this term is appropriate to certain internal changes in evangelical faith, the
most noticeable of which are the growth in scholarship, the
renewal in social concern, and the more sophisticated political understanding which is developing.

BORN AGAIN! [7]

The most significant—and overlooked—religious phenomenon of the 1970s [is] the emergence of evangelical
Christianity into a position of respect and power. "There
is a hidden religious power base in American culture which
our secular biases prevent many of us from noticing," says
Catholic theologian and writer Michael Novak. "Jimmy
Carter has found it.". . .

Evangelicalism is the religion you get when you "get"
religion. Its substance and style vary by region, denomination and theological tradition. But all evangelicals are
united by a subjective experience of personal salvation,
which they describe as being "born again," converted or regenerated.

[7] Excerpts from article by Kenneth L. Woodward, religion editor, with John
Barnes and Laurie Lisle, *Newsweek* writers. *Newsweek.* 88:68–70+, 0. 25, '76.

The term *evangelical* derives from the Greek word *euangelion,* meaning "good news," which American evangelicals are committed to spread through preaching and proselytizing. Unlike most other Christians, evangelicals insist that all people must be converted to Christ before they can do anything in their lives that is pleasing to God. They are Protestants who take a conservative view of Christian doctrine, emphasize personal morality rather than social ethics, look to the Bible as the sole authority in faith and practice and tend to regard themselves as the only true heirs of the New Testament church. As one evangelical church proudly proclaims on its cornerstone: "The church of Christ. Founded in Jerusalem in A.D. 33. Established in Sweetwater, Texas, A.D. 1928."

Evangelicals can be found in every part of the country and in virtually every Protestant denomination. They are particularly strong among the Southern Baptists who constitute the dominant church of the Deep South. Across the border states and into the Great Plains, where circuit-riders once preached, evangelicals can be encountered in the Wesleyan, Holiness and Methodist congregations. Thanks to revivalism, the conservative Baptists are prospering in the Pacific Northwest, and many Missouri Synod Lutherans in the Midwest share the evangelical view of biblical authority.

The folkways of evangelicalism vary as much as its geography. In the Middle West, the initial approach to "embrace Jesus" may be nothing more than a neighborly knock at the door, followed by an invitation to "fellowship" at a church supper or a businessmen's Wednesday morning prayer breakfast. Effusiveness is not the Northerners' style, but they will attend an outdoor evangelistic crusade and stand up for Jesus Christ during a half-time tribute at a football game.

In the South, religion is traditionally a more demonstrative affair, and revivalism is a form of people's theater. In their gospel music, black churches enrich the evangelical tradition with their own experience of oppression and audi-

bly encourage their preachers to "say it, brother." Although
tents still go up in rural towns and some converts trek to
creeks for baptism by total immersion, established Southern
Baptist churches have grown more reserved and ritualistic.
Churches still mount crusades for Christ, but now much of
the drama of salvation is played out on television. There,
preachers like Jim Bakker plead for converts to call in,
charismatics ask viewers to touch their TV sets to receive
God's power, and emcees interview celebrities like Watergate veteran Charles Colson to hear what good God has
wrung out of past wrongdoing. In the booming evangelical
book market, the message is the same: not a call to Christian servanthood, but an upbeat stress on what God's power
can do for you. . . .

Divisions Still Exist

Despite the evangelicals' newfound strength, a number
of serious divisions have opened up within their ranks.
Evangelicals are sharply divided over fundamental religious
issues such as the infallibility of Scripture and what they
think the Gospel requires of them as born-again Christians.
Searching for more authentic Christian life-styles, younger
evangelicals are rejecting the salvation-brings-success ethos
of establishment evangelicals. And in their hour of political
ascendancy, the evangelicals are exhibiting new and often
sharply divergent views on how the church should relate
to public affairs.

For the first time in this century, large numbers of
evangelicals are stepping out of cultural isolation and as-
suming the burdens of political responsibility once exercised largely by mainline Protestants in consort with Jewish
and Catholic leaders. Evangelicals have, with few exceptions, looked upon politics as part of a corrupt, unregen-
erate world that Christians ought to avoid. To be sure,
evangelicals have always influenced local politics wherever
their numbers have given them the leverage of social pressure. In Georgia, for example, an evangelical coalition is
currently leading opposition to a bill that would legalize

bingo, a change favored by the state's Catholic minority. Only recently, however, have evangelical majorities begun to recognize politics as a more positive exercise of power. . . .

The . . . [1976 presidential campaign] also brought to the fore some of the deep-seated cultural differences between the Southern Baptists, as the South's dominant religious group, and the Northern evangelical establishment as represented by the National Association of Evangelicals (which claims to include 3.5 million Protestants), the National Religious Broadcasters, the Billy Graham Evangelistic Association and *Christianity Today* magazine, the unofficial voice of established evangelical opinion. These organizations were brought into being within the last 35 years by Northern fundamentalists who opposed the liberal drift of mainline Protestant denominations but who also wanted to adopt a somewhat more open, challenging stance toward modern society than old-fashioned fundamentalists were willing to take. They appropriated the label "evangelical," which in recent years has become synonymous with "conservative Protestant."

Compared to the effusive Southerners, the Northern evangelical spokesmen are wintry in temperament, scrupulously scholastic—and largely Calvinistic—in intellectual style, and invariably conservative in their social and political positions. They have tried for decades to unite evangelicals behind their own doctrinal stance and regularly include the Southern Baptists when describing the boundaries of their projected evangelical empire. But the Southern Baptists enjoy their exclusivity. And when editor Harold Lindsell of *Christianity Today* recently took to the pulpit to twice cast doubt on Jimmy Carter's religious commitment as a "born-again Christian," some Southern Baptist officials insisted that they never had belonged to the evangelical camp.

"We are *not* evangelicals," says Foy Valentine, the liberal activist who has long headed the SBC's [Southern Baptist Convention's] Christian Life Commission. "That's a Yankee word. They want to claim us because we are big and

successful and growing every year. But we have our own
traditions, our own hymns and more students in our seminaries than they have in all of theirs put together. We don't
share their politics or their fussy fundamentalism, and we
don't want to get involved in their theological witch-
hunts." . . .

According to historian Martin Marty, the foremost in-
terpreter of modern American religion, the . . . [recent] history of American Protestantism is the story of conflict
between two parties—proponents of "public" Protestantism
and advocates of "private" Protestantism. The former
adopted the optimistic view that Christians can and should
change society through social reform, ecumenism and moral
influence on secular learning, leaders and politics. Although
the optimism of public Protestantism receded after World
War I, its sobered shadow still fires the outlook of mainline
Protestant churches.

In contrast, private Protestants have adopted the pesi-
mistic view that the world is an evil place from which revivalists must rescue souls one by one. For a century, this
essentially American outlook has been colored by fundamentalist assumptions that the Apocalypse is near; only
after Christ's return in glory, so this interpretation of Scripture runs, will there be a just society. This view still dominates the more fundamentalist schools, such as Dallas
Theological Seminary and the Moody Bible Institute in
Chicago.

As the chief exponents of private Protestantism, revivalists since Dwight L. Moody have traditionally preached
against liberal social reform, as if they expected Christ himself to return as a self-made man. This bond between revivalism and social conservatism has led to some interesting
alliances. Tracing the lineage of popular revivalists from
Moody through Billy Sunday to Billy Graham, evangelical
historian Richard Pierard has compiled a list of wealthy
patrons who have always been the mainstays of mass evangelism. . . .

For many younger evangelicals, private Protestantism's

dependence upon conservative patronage helps to explain what sociologist David Moberg calls "the Great Reversal"— the loss of that zeal that propelled many born-again believers of the old evangelicalism into the forefront of the movements for abolition and women's suffrage. Embarrassed by the evangelical establishment's opposition to the civil-rights, peace and anti-poverty movements of the 1960s, the younger believers are re-examining the social teachings of the Bible—and of other Christian traditions—in the hope of closing the gap between private and public demonstrations of their faith.

With typical evangelical fervor, groups of "New Evangelicals" are asserting alternate forms of leadership. Beginning in 1973 with its historic "Chicago Declaration," an ecumenical group of scholars and activists called "Evangelicals for Social Action," has functioned as a goad to repentance, reform and radical social witness within the wider evangelical community. "Daughters of Sarah," a monthly newsletter, and the Evangelical Women's Caucus now offer a biblically based feminism to combat the sexism they find in church and in the popular marriage guide, *The Total Woman.* And on evangelical campuses, such as Wheaton College in Illinois, students are devouring books by New Evangelical spokesmen like Sen. Mark Hatfield of Oregon, whose scriptural defense of political liberalism is new to most evangelical ears.

All these themes find exposure in *Sojourners,* a monthly magazine of radical Christian opinion published in Washington, D.C. In a rare departure for evangelical journals, *Sojourners* combines tough investigative reporting with uncompromising commitment to biblical imperatives. More important, the editors regularly feature other radical Christians, such as the Catholic Workers' Dorothy Day and Mennonite scholar John Howard Yoder, whose deep spirituality and dogged Christian discipleship provide models for evangelicals. "We think that evangelical Christians can be found wherever anyone chooses the Cross as a way of life," says editor Jim Wallis. "We think that Christians must count the cost of conversion and recognize that the way of Jesus is a radical alternative to the values of our society."

Evangelical Christianity has been growing quietly for ten years—often at the expense of played-out mainline churches. During that period, evangelicals have zealously sought out the young, offering the certainties of a fired-up faith as an alternative to secular disillusion. But as it happens, just as the nation is at last taking notice of their strength, evangelicals find their house divided. The Presidential election has only exacerbated latent differences in doctrine and social attitudes. As a result, 1976 may yet turn out to be the year that the evangelicals won the White House but lost cohesiveness as a distinct force in American religion and culture.

CHARISMATIC CHRISTIANS [8]

Shouts of "Hallelujah!" and "Praise the Lord!" resound through cavernous convention halls as thousands of jubilant Christians cast arms and eyes upward. Many wear fixed, faraway stares and others gently sway as they sing such hymns as "Come Holy Ghost."

As they move about, they greet each other excitedly, often embracing and punctuating conversations with "Glory to God!" and "Amen!" Crowded into Arrowhead Stadium [in Kansas City, Missouri] to hear messages of inspiration and exortation, they can gaze toward the electronic signboard which emblazens the message "Jesus Is Lord."

With other Christians this multitude of the faithful, 50,000 gathered . . . in the largest such meeting ever held, believe fervently in Christ's power to save lost souls. But they are also animated by conviction not shared by all Christians: an ardent belief that their lives have been dramatically changed by an infusion of the Holy Spirit of God. . . .

[8] From " 'Charismatic Christians' Seek to Infuse the Faith With Their Joyous Spirit," by Kenneth A. Briggs, staff writer. New York *Times*. p. B 1. Jl. 22, '77. © 1977 by the New York Times Company. Reprinted by permission.

This has led them to some practices that are hailed as signs of a great new undertaking by God to renew Christianity. They contend that through their faith they are empowered by the Spirit to do such supernatural acts as healing the sick and uttering prophecies.

The most controversial "gift" that is supposed to be given by the Spirit is "speaking in tongues," an exotic practice by which the Spirit is believed to speak through a convert in unknown languages.

Known variously as Pentecostals and charismatics, these Christians represent the most vigorous, burgeoning force in American religion today. Followers include men and women of all ages and economic conditions, though most who have come here appear to be relatively affluent. Arriving in busloads, cars and campers from every section of the country, they display crosses and Bibles and some wear Jesus T-shirts, they are ebullient and confident of being the vanguard of the sweeping spiritual trend.

The movement takes its roots in the miraculous events recounted in the New Testament that took place on the 50th day after Christ's Resurrection, or Pentecost Sunday. Tradition holds that on that day the Spirit of Christ came among His followers. The word *charisma*, taken from the Greek root "charis," meaning grace, is held to be the access to divine power given to every Christian but not realized by all.

In terms of ecumenical cooperation and the advance of the charismatic movement, this sprawling rally is breaking new ground and is another sign of the evangelical fervor that marks the movement.

Christians from a broad spectrum of denominations, including Roman Catholics, Mennonites and Baptists, have organized behind the effort and have put their differences aside to an unusual extent to foster common beliefs.

In so doing, the event mirrors the charismatic style in thousands of American communities where those who describe themselves as "born in the Spirit" transcend denominational ties in common prayer groups and Bible study.

The present surge of Pentacostalism represents the second great expansion in the movement since its distinctive practices were introduced at the turn of the century.

Initially the movement was a protest against what many considered the cultural conformity and middle-class respectability of established Protestantism. Its appeal was particularly strong among the poor. Several churches, including the Assemblies of God, which has a membership of 1.3 million, were formed in this period.

The second stage began in the early 1960s and has attracted large numbers of affluent Christians, many of whom remain members of mainstream churches while participating in nonparochial neo-Pentecostal groupings. Most prefer the term *charismatic* to distinguish themselves from independent Pentecostals, who have formed new churches or joined older ones.

Most observers attribute the spectacular growth of the charismatic movement to a combination of conditions, among them the presence of a widespread desire for close, transforming experiences with God and a longing for worship that encourages self-expression.

Members of the so-called "classical" Pentecostal churches that arose earlier in the century are estimated to number four million in this country. Another million or so people have identified with the current phase of the movement, of whom 70 percent are Catholic.

Underground Groups Disappearing

Gauging the size and scope of Pentecostalism is made difficult by the free-flowing nature of much of the movement. In addition, some members of established churches, eager to avoid possible disapproval by those churches, have taken part in somewhat underground groups. As the movement has gained acceptability, this tendency has largely disappeared.

Based on approximate figures supplied by the heads of charismatic groups within mainstream churches, there are roughly 40,000 Presbyterians and 20,000 Baptists in the movement. One trend noted by most observers is that, within Protestant ranks, followers are more likely to be clergy while the Catholic wing is overwhelmingly lay. For instance, 29 percent of Episcopal priests receive the Episcopal charismatic newsletter.

In the 10 years since a group of students and faculty from Duquesne University in Pittsburgh launched the Catholic "charismatic renewal," the movement has become a major element in the church, and the hierarchy, often with certain wariness, has cautiously endorsed it.

One source of uneasiness among bishops is the suspicion that the movement's free-wheeling ways could disrupt church order and that its inclination to respond above all to the call of the spirit could undercut ecclesiastical authority.

The crowning act of legitimacy took place on Pentecost Sunday in 1975 in St. Peter's Basilica when Pope Paul VI warmly praised the activities of a throng of charismatic Catholics who had made a special pilgrimage to the Vatican.

For all its success as a grass-roots phenomenon across the nation, the movement has also drawn sharp criticism from those who consider its methods and emphases unbiblical and even harmful.

The 2.8-million-member Lutheran Church-Missouri Synod, a bastion of evangelical conservatism, has repeatedly condemned the movement, contending that it falsely exalts personal experience over the authority of the Bible and that it down-grades the role of Christ in the process of salvation.

Ministers in the synod have been dismissed for embracing Pentecostalism, as have clergy in other denominations.

Other critics focus scorn on the movement's intense emotionalism and its tendency to produce cults around strong-willed personalities.

For example, the independent *National Catholic Reporter,* while applauding the movement's ability to rejuvenate many lapsed Catholics and to spur spiritual renewal, also warned in a recent editorial that the movement contained elements of "narcissism" and that it was sometimes "inward and narrow." . . .

Over the past decade, as new independent churches have sprung up and others have begun groups within existing denominations, charismatics have created a network of personal contacts and a common spiritual language that overcomes traditional religious boundaries. Moreover, as a minority movement in American religion, movement member churches have shared books, speakers and meeting grounds.

The [July 1977] gathering . . . [in Kansas City] manifests the highest level of ecumenism yet attained by the movement, though that was not the direct goal. Altogether 10 district groupings of Christians, with the approval of their church leadership, . . . [are taking] part.

Ironically, the largest single group, the Assemblies of God, . . . [is] not officially . . . [participating]. For the most part, the older, established pentecostal churches are the most virulently fundamentalistic and remain largely unwilling to have contact with other churches.

PRESIDENT CARTER'S RELIGION [9]

The word *evangelical* first came into wide use with [Martin] Luther. It was the generic term for Christ-believing non-Catholics in this country until the end of the 19th century, when the pressure of Darwinism split Protestants into two camps: the liberals, who questioned the absolute historical accuracy of the Bible and formalized the Christian practice of charity into the "Social Gospel," and the fundamentalists, who insisted that personal salvation was the sole purpose of Christian faith and held that five "fundamentals" (biblical inerrancy plus the virgin birth, the

[9] From "An Ex-Believer Defends Carter's Religion," by Robert Christgau, senior editor. *Village Voice.* 31:11-13. Ag. 16, '76. Reprinted by permission of *The Village Voice.* Copyright © The Village Voice, Inc., 1976.

necessity of Christ's physical atonement for sin on the
cross, the bodily resurrection of Christ, and the second
coming) were essential to that faith. Many fundamentalists
also believed in "premillennial dispensationalism," which
dismissed as futile any attempt to achieve worldly progress
until the time of Christ's return. With its tendency to put
doctrine above spirit, its resistance to biblical criticism,
and its general reputation for boobishness, fundamentalism
was on the defensive almost continually. But in 1944, a
more scholarly, less rigid Protestant conservatism began to
be articulated in the newly formed National Association
of Evangelicals. These new evangelicals tended to be more
confident because they were more at home in the world;
they could provide an old-time religion that wasn't so
shrilly unmodern. Under clergy trained in this tradition,
membership in denominations opposed to the liberal ecu-
menicism of the mainline churches has surged, as has
membership in newer conservative denominations and
charismatic sects. As of now, Jimmy Carter's religion is the
fastest-growing in the country.

Yet despite its intellectual respectability (because of it,
in a way), I don't think the term "evangelical" indicates
very accurately what 30 million, or 40 million, or 50 million—I've encountered all three figures more than once—
members of hundreds of American sects and denominations and thousands of independent churches share with
Jimmy Carter. I almost prefer its cognate "evangelistic,"
which recalls by implication all the great awakenings and
revivals that have renewed American popular religion over
three centuries. The problem with "evangelical" is that
it's not homely enough; many of Carter's coreligionists
don't use it. Quite a few, including many Southern Baptists, still prefer "fundamentalist." Among blacks, whose
link of faith with Carter is the secret of their passionate
support, the favored term is "Bible-believing." And while
"conservative" is a precise if colorless theological alternative, its political connotations don't much suit the likes of
Jim Wallis, a former antiwar activist who edits a magazine

for "biblical people" called *Sojourners*. *Sojourners* devoted much of its April issue to "a disclosure of an alarming political initiative by the evangelical far right" led by Arizona Congressman John Conlan.

Nevertheless, with all differences granted, these 30 or 40 or 50 million people are definitely united—by a common allegiance, an allegiance often described as "a personal relationship with Jesus Christ." To secular humanists such a phrase sounds mystical and quite out of time, and thus frightening. Or so it is said. Perhaps what's really frightening is its populist thrust—intellectuals always feel threatened when the unsophisticated define their own philosophical prerogatives. The Calvinists who founded conservative Christianity in this country would not have countenanced such chummy talk about the Son of God; for them, the doctrine of salvation by grace meant that one's redemption by Christ was at the whim of the Almighty. But just as the mass revivalism that proved essential to religious fervor in a land so vast and fruitful often operated beyond ecclesiastical authority, so it brought home the individual's responsibility—or "ability" as it was often called—in receiving grace. It has been a recurrent theme of Jimmy Carter's kind of Christianity that any person—regardless of church of birth or past sins or beliefs about angels and pins—can be born again and achieve salvation by accepting Christ into his or her heart.

This act of acceptance and rebirth, the conversion experience, is not, properly speaking, mystical; it doesn't normally involve visions or seizures. Perhaps the best way of explaining it to skeptics is to call it a turning point—a time of crisis and self-doubt that may last days, months, even years, before it is brought to an end by an emotional resolve that transforms a person's consciousness, sometimes for a whole lifetime. Even skeptics have turning points, and although born-again Christians will no doubt feel belittled by the comparison, in practice that's what a conversion experience is like. Christians interpret it as the forgiveness of sin by God and often claim a permanent joy as a result. They acknowledge, however, that they do still experience doubt and unhappiness; their joy in the knowledge of Christ manifests itself as a substratum of purpose and confidence that gets them through.

Usually conversion is sudden and distinct, but sometimes it's not—many young Christians go through adolescence wondering whether this or that momentary rush was It, then settle into adulthood somehow convinced they are saved. That is the way it seems to have been for Jimmy Carter. He had what he regarded as a conversion experience as a boy of 11, but that was not why he felt moved to start teaching Sunday school at 18, and later became a church deacon active in Southern Baptist affairs throughout his region of south Georgia. His church responsibilities were a natural consequence of his status and ambitions—not ordained, certainly, but hardly unexpected. By the time he was 42, a two-term state senator who had just barely lost a dark-horse race for governor, his public piety ensured no more than that he was a typical American politician.

Sociologists of religion are fond of pointing out that the conversion experience often takes place during normal times of crisis—especially at puberty, but also around the change of life in middle age. Carter's real Christian turning point occurred after he lost the governor's race in 1966. Bitterly disappointed, he found himself questioning the depth of his Christian commitment, and was finally led to rededicate his life to Christ by his sister, Ruth Carter Stapleton. Stapleton is often described as a faith healer, which is meant to imply either charlatan or nut, but that conjures up images that are much too outlandish. In her book, *The Gift of Inner Healing*, she sounds more like a California encounter therapist who happens to be born again—characteristically, she induces the subject to imagine his or her "traumatic experience" and then insert the all-forgiving figure of Christ into the picture (after which one can almost hear her saying, "All better"). But however fatuous her calling may seem, the counsel she gave her brother might have come from any responsive member of the evangelical clergy. She told him he would never find peace until he had put Christ before everything else in his life—even his political ambitions. He resisted at first, but finally agreed.

The root of Carter's conversion experience might have been "psychological," but (as is so often true of comparable conversions to radical politics) it had genuine spiritual and behavioral results. By the following June, he had become a zealous part-time saver of souls. Where previously he had congratulated himself for a witness comprising a few house calls before revival week in Plains, he now traveled to several northern slums to help the unfortunate find the Lord. This is impressive. I recall from my own experience (and I grant that Carter's was very different: I was a callow youth when I considered myself saved, and I did not grow up in a place where my religion was considered the norm) that there is no more trying Christian duty than witnessing to nonbelievers. Many church members avoid it entirely. Not only is it time-consuming, it is embarrassing; it requires a rare inner confidence that springs only from intense belief.

Carter makes clear in his autobiography that his rediscovery of Christ, coinciding with the only major failure of his life, represented a partial victory over the sin that haunts him: spiritual pride. This is a common sin among politicians, and I have been told by both non-Baptist Southerners and non-Baptist evangelicals that it is a common sin among Southern Baptists, but in Carter it seems to transcend such parameters. . . . In the humble quiet of his public presence, Carter tries to suggest that he is mostly past his own self-righteousness, but succeeds only in conveying that it's still a problem.

REASONS FOR EVANGELICAL GROWTH [10]

If I believed that the religious reawakening of America's evangelicals, spurred by the election of one of their number to the presidency, would lead to a wave of intolerance toward those of other beliefs, I would be apprehensive. But I think the consequences are likely to be the opposite.

What is taking place among white, working-class evangelical Protestants is largely a reflection of the increasing self-awareness and cultural consciousness that occurred somewhat earlier among America's Jews, blacks, and Catholics. The election of a Roman Catholic president [John F. Kennedy] sixteen years ago did not increase religious polarization; it substantially lessened it. The emergence of capable and forceful black leaders, like Martin Luther King, and a growing circle of black mayors and members of Congress has not increased black-white confrontation. On the contrary, by demonstrating the intelligence and capability of blacks in positions of influence, these new leaders enable people of both races to meet more easily in an atmosphere of mutual recognition and respect.

Some may not accept the comparison as valid. They may argue that Jews, Catholic ethnics, and blacks were handicapped minorities only coming into possession of civil rights long enjoyed by America's evangelical Protestants, who were the oppressors and overlords. To some degree this perception is true, but it is partial and misleading.

America's fundamentalists and evangelicals have been, in many respects, our nation's least visible ethnic and social minority. Although Protestants as a whole constitute two-thirds of the population, the evangelicals, such as Jimmy Carter's Southern Baptists, do not. We must remember that Protestantism in America is little more than a catch-all label of uncertain meaning for virtually everyone

[10] From "A Dynamic Religious Diversity," by Edward L. Ericson, chairman, Board of Leaders, New York Society for Ethical Culture. *Humanist.* 37:37. Ja./F. '77. This article first appeared in *The Humanist* January/February 1977 and is reprinted by permission.

who is not specifically Jewish, Catholic, or an adherent of the statistically minor non-Christian beliefs, such as Islam or Buddhism.

Public-opinion surveys over the past few years have shown that 65 to 66 percent of Americans think of themselves as Protestant, but many of this number are religiously inactive or unaffiliated. Moreover, these "Protestants" range in belief from humanistic Unitarians and liberal Congregationalists to ultra-fundamentalists, such as Jehovah's Witnesses and Seventh Day Adventists—who in turn are not regarded as orthodox by other conservative Protestants. A Christian Scientist, a liberal Methodist, and an observant Mormon have very little in common in matters of faith except a general cultural heritage and a biblical literature that they understand in radically different ways. . . .

The statistics show that during the past quarter-century traditional Christian supernaturalism has neither grown nor declined.

What we are observing is the greater visibility of evangelical subcultures that, until recently, had remained isolated in the so-called Bible Belt of the rural South and Midwest. We are witnessing the emergence of millions of poor, less-educated working-class people, both black and white, into the mainstream of American life. Many of them, like President . . . Carter, have overcome the isolation of a provincial and regional culture; an increasing number represent the first generation in their families to go to college, to travel, or to work with people of other cultural and regional backgrounds.

In the process of becoming more cosmopolitan and informed, some are leaving their historical family religions for one of the more liberal churches, or becoming unaffiliated. But many others, like Mr. Carter, are choosing to maintain their religious ties and are able to find a transforming spiritual integrity in them. Even so, when one reads Mr. Carter's description of the ethical and religious philosophers who have influenced his religious consciousness, figures that include Niebuhr, Tillich, and the heretical Russian mystic, Tolstoy—who also influenced Gandhi and the civil-rights movement—it is apparent that Carter's religious consciousness is much more supple and subtle than that of the narrow and xenophobic fundamentalist—and this leavening of the evangelical loaf will be an increasing phenomenon.

Therefore, on balance, I do not share the misgivings of those who seem to fear that a resurgent Christian supernaturalism is about to overwhelm respect for humanistic values and the scientific method. The evangelical and fundamentalist churches are growing—within historically limited boundaries—for two reasons: (1) the main-line churches have become substantially more cosmopolitan and secular in recent decades with the result that many of their less adaptable members are transferring their allegiance to groups that have changed more slowly; and (2) like other populations in transition, the formerly rural working-class populations that have moved recently into urban life have strengthened their ties with their ancestral churches as a way of cushioning a world of bewildering change. These are the groups most distressed by change and most likely to experience economic insecurity and social dislocation. Their traditional religious faith answers a real need for stability and a sense of identity in their lives.

It seems to me compatible with a rational and humanistic outlook to understand this need and to treat it sympathetically. It is a self-limiting adjustment and not likely to be the wave of the future—unless humanists [who exalt the cultural and rational aspects of man, rather than the supernatural] become self-indulgent and thus discredit the moral and intellectual commitment we are perceived as representing.

III. THE CATHOLIC CHURCH IN AMERICA

EDITOR'S INTRODUCTION

Religious change in the United States is nowhere more obvious and more deeply felt than in the Roman Catholic Church. Before 1962 most Americans—whether Catholic or not—thought of the Catholic Church as "a spiritual fortress," to quote the feature story from *Time* that opens this section. But remarkable developments have occurred since then. From 1962 through 1965, bishops and other Church officials gathered in Rome for the Second Vatican Council, or Vatican II as it is also known. Out of the council's deliberations came changes in practice and attitude, if not in belief, that have profoundly affected Catholics everywhere, and most particularly in the United States. In addition, of course, the Catholic Church has been affected over the past two decades by the same social and political conditions that have left their mark on other religions.

Reports from *Newsweek* and the New York *Times* relate some of the discussion and action, particularly on social issues in the Catholic Church today. Concluding this section are two articles that draw widely differing conclusions concerning the state of Catholicism in America today.

A DIVIDED CHURCH [1]

Roman Catholic. The words are redolent of rich and solemn rituals chanted amid clouds of incense in an ancient tongue. Many American Catholics over 30 remember living in that history-heavy church as if living in a spiritual fortress—comforting at times, inhibiting and even

[1] From "A Church Divided." *Time.* 197:48–50+. My. 24 '76. Reprinted by permission from *Time,* the Weekly Newsmagazine; Copyright Time, Inc. 1976.

terrifying at others. But it was a safe and ordered universe, with eternal guarantees for those who lived by its rules.

That fortress has crumbled. Before the Second Vatican Council in 1962, the U.S. Catholic Church had seemed, at least to outsiders, to be a monolith of faith, not only the church's richest province but, arguably, its most pious. When the council ended in 1965, American Catholicism had been swept by a turbulent new mood, a mood of opened windows, tumbled walls, broken chains. It became a painful experience for many, and over the next decade the casualties were heavy: nuns leaving their convents, priests their ministries, lay Catholics simply walking away from worship and belief.

The American Catholic Church in 1976—by far the largest U.S. denomination, with nearly 49 million members—is a less tumultuous church, its attrition slowed. But it is still a questing and divided church, troubled by colliding purposes and visions. An increasing number of lay people (themselves split on such issues as social action and piety, tradition and change) call themselves Catholic but are resentful of the church's authority over their private lives. Bishops differ markedly on the nature of their role and in the exercise of their power. Priests, nuns and brothers are now on one side, now the other. . . .

Nowhere is the division more spectacular than on the issue of birth control. In 1968 Pope Paul VI issued his encyclical *Humanae vitae,* explicitly telling Catholics they were forbidden to use artificial methods of contraception. In 1974 a study of American Catholics showed that fully 83% did not accept such teaching. Moreover, attendance at weekly Mass dropped from 71% in 1963 to 50% in 1974; monthly confession, from 38% to 17%.

Those figures—and a theory to explain them—appeared this spring in a new book called *Catholic Schools in a Declining Church* by priest-sociologist Andrew Greeley and his colleagues at Chicago's National Opinion Research Center, William C. McCready and Kathleen McCourt. Their conclusion: *Humanae vitae* created a massive crisis of authority in the church. An ethical mandate from the Pope, promulgated by his bishops, was quietly—if not without some qualms of conscience—rejected by Catholic families. In turn, there were empty pews in church, no more lines at the confessional.

The Greeley theory has been sharply questioned by some other scholars, by churchmen, and by people who cannot forget that Greeley is also a sharp-penned journalist. But many Catholics agree that *Humanae vitae* was, at the very least, a blow that shattered rising expectations for change. The Second Vatican Council had signaled to Catholics that they might have more freedom than they once thought. The crucial Declaration on Religious Freedom (largely the work of American Jesuit John Courtney Murray) stated that religious liberty was a human right—an admission the church had never before made. It was by no means intended to give Catholics carte blanche to disagree with their church, but with *Humanae vitae,* they did.

There is of course plenty of other evidence—and there are other theories—about decline and division in the church. The annual Official Catholic Directories have been carrying the statistics of decline throughout the decade. The figures show that about 3,100 Catholic elementary and high schools, out of 13,340, have closed in the past ten years, and enrollment has dropped from 5.6 million in 1965 to 3.5 million in 1975.

Some 35,000 American nuns and 10,000 priests—even a brilliant bishop—left their ministries, and sometimes even the church, in a great exodus. Some of them left explicitly to marry, others out of disillusionment or loss of faith, still others because they believed they could serve God or humanity more effectively in the then celebrated "secular city." There are fewer new priests to replace those who left. Seminary enrollment, at a high of nearly 49,000 in 1964, fell to a low of 17,200 in 1975. Only this year has there been a modest upturn—an increase of some 800—indicating that the trend may have bottomed out.

The departures of lay Catholics are less frequent now,

but there were many. Some succumbed to what Greeley calls the "meat on Friday" syndrome. (The practice of abstaining from meat on Friday, meant to emulate Jesus' fasting and to commemorate the day he was crucified, eventually became a church commandment and for centuries served as a kind of Roman Catholic badge.) "Once it became legitimate [in 1966] to eat meat on Friday, one could doubt the authority of the Pope, practice birth control, leave the priesthood and get married or indeed do anything else one wanted to," he writes. Although he rejects this factor as a major explanation of the religious fall-off, certain Catholics found it painfully real. . . .

Another sign of disaffection: the divorce rate among American Catholics is approaching that of non-Catholics. As one result, diocesan marriage tribunals have been examining an increasing number of broken marriages, and last year granted almost 10,000 annulments—declarations that a sacramental marriage never existed. . . .

But even Catholics who are liberal on marital and sexual issues can be adamant about abortion—at least for themselves and their families. "Abortion is murder to me," says Mary Ann Murphy, 54, of Alexandria, Va. "But I cannot jam my religious beliefs down someone else's throat." Jan Slevin, a nurse, refused to work in the obstetrics unit of Washington General Hospital because of the many abortions performed there. "In a case of incest, rape or some psychological trauma," she concedes, "I can see a morning-after pill or a shot to prevent pregnancy. But I think abortion is morally evil. It is a taking of life."

Matters of Rite and Wrong

The furor stirred up by the most visible reform inspired by Vatican II—the modernizing of the rites of worship, most notably the Mass—seems to have largely died down. In the years following the council, the language of the liturgy became English, not Latin; baroque high altars gave way to simple tables; members of what had once jokingly been called "the church of silence" were urged to sing hymns—

and often Protestant ones at that (a familiar favorite these days: [Martin] Luther's *A Mighty Fortress Is Our God*). Instead of incense and plain chant, parish churches now offered folk Masses, Masses with "sacred dancing," mixed-media Masses. . . .

Thousands of Catholics still mourn the disappearance of the old Latin . . . Mass. (In fact, it is still celebrated—illicitly—by a few rebel priests, like Father Gommar De Pauw of Westbury, N.Y.) . . . Some Catholics find the new rite too cluttered with movement, hymns and communal prayers. . . .

Still, the majority of U.S. Catholics are comfortable with the new liturgies. Greeley's study found that more than 80% approved or even preferred the new rites. "When I was a kid, you didn't understand what was happening in Mass," remembers Janet Tambascio, a young mother who grew up in St. Columbkille's parish in Brighton, Mass. "You played with your rosary beads, which had nothing to do with anything. Now we aren't just sitting in Mass; we're participating."

One virtue of the new rite of worship is its flexibility. Priests now celebrate the Eucharist [the symbolic receiving of bread and wine] in homes, offices and hotels for small groups, as well as in churches. This freedom has allowed innovative clergymen to extend their ministry in intriguing new ways. St. Louis parish in Miami offers a Mass that uses young people in adult capacities—reading the Epistle and Gospel, acting as ushers, leading the music. In East Los Angeles, priests from Our Lady of Solitude parish celebrate Mass in the area's housing projects for members of *barrio* gangs who are fearful of crossing another gang's turf to get to church. And not very far away, in Orange County, Father Don Duplessis conducts home Masses once a month for a group of singles who call themselves the Orange County Catholic Alumni Club. "Here you don't feel out of place," said a participant at one of the singles' Masses last month. "When you go to Mass in church, everything is so family-oriented. You are always the one to walk in alone, stand alone and keep very much alone."

Catholics are still adjusting to another reform, the "new" rite of penance, renamed the sacrament of reconciliation, which was put into effect in most U.S. parishes this past Lenten season. It is now a longer process often involving face-to-face easy-chair conversation between penitent and priest, although those who prefer it can retain the anonymity of the old screened confessional....

There are no round-the-corner lines yet for the new penitential rite. But the failure to confess does not keep people away from Communion, as it once did. Churches across the U.S. report an increase in the proportion of their worshipers who receive weekly Communion—from about one-fifth of them a decade ago to more than half today. One possible reason: the newer Catholic teaching suggests that it is hard—not easy—for a reasonably religious person to commit mortal sins, the principal impediment that would keep someone from Communion....

Despite the slight rebound in the numbers of new seminarians this year, the church still faces a serious vocation crisis; already in some dioceses there are not enough priests to go around. That prospect may be partly responsible for a growing and yet unresolved debate over two alternatives that for the moment are unacceptable to the hierarchy; women priests and married priests.

Heads of women's religious orders, other nuns, laywomen—some 1,200 in all—met in Detroit last November to discuss and coordinate their cause. Says Elizabeth Carroll, a Sister of Mercy working at Washington's Center of Concern: "The arguments for women in the priesthood are unassailable." The bishops do not agree. Archbishop Joseph L. Bernardin [president of the National Conference of Catholic Bishops] argues that "serious theological objections" still stand in the way of women priests. [See "Women as Episcopal Priests," in Section IV, below.] ...

What may come sooner than the ordination of women is the option for priests to marry—or at least for some mar-

ried men to become priests. But Pope Paul has no intention
of easing the rule of clerical celibacy, and some lay Catholics
have misgivings too.

A Dilemma for Pope and Bishop

Theoretically, authority in the church is exercised by
the Pope in conjunction with his bishops. Time was when
decrees of the Pontiff or the hierarchy on any issue were
obediently accepted by Catholic Americans, as if they were
the laws of God. No longer. In matters of faith as well as
morals, Catholics seem to be making up their own minds.
The Greeley study, for example, shows that only 37% of
U.S. Catholics fully accept the doctrine of the infallibility
of the Pope—a dogma solemnly defined by the First Vatican
Council in 1870. . . .

For the American bishops—and perhaps much more
acutely for Pope Paul—it is a dilemma: how to guide those
who seem to need authority without alienating those who
cherish their freedom. Catholic Americans who have met
the Pope in audiences in Rome are almost invariably
touched by the Pope's personal warmth, but that does not
necessarily enhance his credibility. . . .

Seeking a Delicate Balance

What is the future of the U.S. church? Jesuit sociologist
John Thomas is pessimistic about an end to the drift from
the church. "Some like to call the present transition a 'second
spring,' " he observes. "I see it as an Indian summer,
which comes just before winter." Biblical scholar John A.
Miles, writing in *Theology Today*, sees Catholics caught in
a no-win situation. If the church does try to exert some kind
of authority, chances are it will only cause further turmoil
and shrinkage. If it does not, it may remain officially large
but "steadily weaker and more diffuse."

Others, however, believe that those who wanted to leave
the church have left, and that those who remain are more
dedicated. Author Sidney Callahan, who stayed in the
church while her husband left it, sees a new spirit of volun-

tarism among Catholics who "want to make the church work." Bishop James Rausch, General Secretary of the U.S. Catholic Conference, feels that the church is entering "a time of healing."

That may be. While the church as an institution still faces formidable problems, Catholics as a people are displaying a remarkable tenacity these days, a kind of spiritual second wind that suggests that U.S. Catholicism might even be on the verge of a new period of vigor.

SPEAKING UP [2]

In an unprecedented experiment in participation, the U.S. Roman Catholic hierarchy invited more than 1,300 concerned clergy and laymen to a national assembly in Detroit. The purpose of the "call to action" conference was to set priorities for a five-year plan on social issues. After three days of spirited debate and intense political maneuverings [in October 1976], the delegates called on the bishops to take several bold steps, some of which seemed certain to surprise—and dismay—the conservative wing of the church. Among the most significant:

Birth Control: Clearly affirm the "right and responsibility" of married Catholics to "form their own consciences" regarding contraception.

Women's Rights: Adopt a two-year plan aimed at allowing women to preach. Seriously study the possibility of ordaining women—and married men—to the priesthood and support an equal rights amendment to the U.S. Constitution.

Divorce: Lift the penalty of automatic excommunication now attached to those Catholics "who dare to remarry after divorce." In addition, publicize those little-known conditions under which remarried Catholics may still receive the church's sacraments.

Economics: Support "full employment" in the U.S.

[2] Reprint of article by Kenneth L. Woodward and James C. Jones. *Newsweek.* 88:110-11. N. 8, '76. Copyright 1976 by Newsweek, Inc. All rights reserved. Reprinted by permission. Woodward is religion editor of *Newsweek*; Jones, a staff writer.

even if this requires massive public employment. Foster research to explore alternative economic structures that will "distribute power more equally." Support the right of prisoners to a minimum wage and urge repeal of existing "right-to-work" laws. Back the rights of agricultural workers as well as employees of all Catholic institutions to form unions.

Discrimination: Eliminate in all institutions of the church every form of discrimination on the basis of "race, language, sex, sexual orientation, culture and mere physical considerations." Support the "concept of open neighborhoods" everywhere.

Amnesty: Support total amnesty for all those Americans who refused to fight the war in Vietnam and abolish all less-than-honorable discharges by the U.S. armed forces.

National Defense: "Lead in resisting" current U.S. policies that abet the proliferation of nuclear weapons and demand a halt to the nation's export of arms.

The resolutions were the result of an unusual exercise in participatory democracy initiated by the U.S. church nearly two years ago as its way of celebrating the nation's Bicentennial. In preparation for the assembly, panels of bishops conducted Congressional-style hearings in six regions of the U.S., listening to grievances from some 450 Catholic members of minority groups—from Mexican migrant workers to American Indians. In addition, 90 dioceses conducted parish-level discussions, the results of which were forwarded to the bishops as part of their efforts to collect grass-roots opinion from the nation's . . . [49] million Catholics.

The assembly itself reflected an equally broad spectrum. Delegates included representatives of 94 Catholic organizations, ranging from the Knights of Columbus to the Slovak Catholic Federation, along with spokesmen for 152 of the nation's 167 dioceses. Responding to the theme of "Liberty and Justice for All," huge majorities supported social positions on which the hierarchy has traditionally taken a liberal stand. Delegates also gave overwhelming approval to the bishops' call for an anti-abortion amendment to the Constitution. On divorce, birth control and the ordination of women, however, the majority's views clearly countered those previously taken by the hierarchy.

Although nearly 100 bishops attended the assembly as voting delegates, the National Conference of Catholic Bishops is not obligated to accept its recommendations. In fact, Archbishop Joseph Bernardin, president of the NCCB, declared last week that the hierarchy's "effort to consult the church at large" had produced only mixed results. "Too much was attempted," said Bernardin, charging that pressure from special-interest groups had produced "a number of recommendations which were not representative of the church in this country." As it happened, most of the delegates were chosen by the bishops themselves. And while the bishops may not welcome all they heard, their ultimate response to the historic assembly probably will determine relations between sheep and shepherds for years to come.

CONFRONTATION AMONG BISHOPS [3]

The Roman Catholic hierarchy in the United States is often seen as a solid fraternity, with personal differences subordinated to the purpose of speaking with a single authoritative voice.

But in recent months, a series of confrontations among bishops has changed this impression of conformity. Leading the way toward change is an emerging nucleus of liberal bishops who are no longer willing to passively tolerate every action taken by the top officers of the hierarchy. Instead, they have begun to form a pressure group to resist policies they oppose.

This mood of independence was exhibited dramatically on Dec. 5 when Bishop Carroll T. Dozier of the Memphis diocese conducted a rite of general absolution aimed at "reconciling" those who were disaffected with the church,

[3] From "Catholic Bishops in the U.S. No Longer Speak in a Single Voice," by Kenneth A. Briggs, staff writer. New York *Times*. sec IV, p 22. Ja. 9, '77. © 1977 by The New York Times Company. Reprinted by permission.

particularly Catholics who are divorced and remarried without ecclesiastical approval. An overflow congregation of 12,000 heard the bishop use a form of penance normally reserved for grave emergencies and welcome them to take communion.

Another sign of independence was shown during the semiannual bishops' meeting in Washington last November when several influential prelates led an emotional, at times acerbic attack on a conventional prepared statement on morality that would have been expected to pass without serious objection a few years ago.

Joining the drive to reject the statement were such prominent figures as Archbishop Peter L. Gerety of Newark, Bishop Francis J. Mugavero of Brooklyn, John Cardinal Dearden of Detroit and Bishop William A. Borders of Baltimore. Though the motion to defeat the statement lost, the dissidents surprisingly picked up more than a fourth of the votes. The debate illustrated the tensions centering on social policy and on the exercise of authority that characterized other disputes during a year of ecclesiastical tumult.

A Welcome Change

For the growing number of liberal bishops, many of them appointed since 1970, the second Vatican council's emphasis on broad consultation at all levels of decision making came as a welcome change from the days when a few powerful cardinals set key policies. Accordingly they espoused the same openness and dialogue among bishops as within parishes and dioceses.

. . . [In 1976] the first evidence of new stirrings among the liberal bishops came during a session of the bishops' administrative council. The body of 50 bishops passed a liberal-inspired document that outlined the political responsibilities of Christians. It was politically nonpartisan and specified such moral concerns as racism, housing and employment. The stage was thus set for a prolonged struggle over priorities which eventually carried directly into the political campaigns of the two major Presidential candidates. Bishop James W. Malone carefully laid out the whole range of Catholic ethical issues outlined by the administrative committee before both Democratic and Republican platform committees. But by the time the candidates met with Archbishop Joseph L. Bernardin, president of the bishops, and his executive committee, the only yardstick used to measure the contenders appeared to be their respective stands on abortion.

In what became a widely quoted set of responses following those meetings, Archbishop Bernardin said he was disappointed with Mr. Carter and encouraged by Mr. Ford. Many bishops were appalled at what seemed to them both a political endorsement and an indefensible simplification of Catholic concerns.

Their anger was vented at a September administrative committee meeting where, in effect, the protest group pressured Archbishop Bernardin to publicly disavow political partisanship and to recognize a broader agenda.

By taking stern disciplinary action that stopped just short of an outright censure of the executive committee, the administrative body, with the key backing of liberal elements, had put the executive committee on notice that it could not take matters into its own hands with impunity.

Less than a month later, the landmark "Call to Action" conference on social action in Detroit became the backdrop for another dramatic clash. [See the preceding article in this section, "Speaking Up."

A Surprising List

Delegates, including bishops, priests, nuns and lay people wrote a surprising list of proposals that urged, among other things, removal of the excommunication penalty from divorced and remarried Catholics, greater stress on the role of conscience in deciding on the means of birth control, and removal of the barriers against women and married men in the priesthood.

Conservative bishops responded warily, fearing that the consultation had gone out of control and appeared to be dictating to the hierarchy. Liberals, on the other hand, were heartened by the Detroit meeting as an advance toward developing national dialogue between the laity and the hierarchy. On doctrinal grounds, they were not far removed from conservatives, remaining loyal to Catholic teaching, but they believed also in the democratic process and the reality of the issues raised by the conference.

The reverberations of the Detroit meeting were very much in the air at the bishops' meeting in November. The clearest evidence was supplied during the debate over the moral statement when several bishops, in arguing against its adoption, said the Detroit proposals should be weighed carefully before any declaration on morality was made.

The liberals believe any approach to morality, particularly to matters of sexual ethics, must take into account the difficulties of Catholics who for one reason or other are out of step with Catholic teaching. They recoil at the didactic, dogmatic language of some church statements that seem to lack compassion for the unfaithful. The experience of the political campaigns and the extraordinary happenings at Detroit appeared to have buoyed them. The Bishops' meeting indicates a new willingness to challenge the conventional ways of the church's ruling class.

VIEWS OF CATHOLICISM TODAY: I [4]

The liturgy began—as it had always begun—when the priest approached the foot of the altar and recited these words. This was the prelude to the unchangeable parts of the Mass of the Catechumens. But the Mass no longer begins this way. These words are no longer spoken. Gone are the sacred Latin high liturgy, the scent of incense, and the sound of bells. The candles no longer burn before the statues of the saints—for the statues have also gone. The faithful Catholic can no longer "go to the altar of God, to

[4] From "The Severed Roots of American Christianity," by Paul Williams, instructor of religious studies, University of Scranton. *National Review.* 28:840-2. Ag. 6, '76. Reprinted by permission of National Review, 150 E. 35th St., New York, N.Y. 10016. (subscription: $19 per year)

God who giveth joy to my youth," for even the altar has
gone. It has been replaced by a "common table."

It is most difficult to remember in these days of meteoric
decline in church membership that less than 15 years ago
more than 80 per cent of the Catholics in America attended
Mass "on a regular basis," in the terminology of the polls,
while nearly 70 per cent of Protestants described themselves
as steady churchgoers. From 1945 to 1965, America was in
the midst of a religious boom. Churches were flooded with
the faithful, and were being constructed at a back-breaking
rate. The Catholic Church alone opened between 150 and
200 new churches each year. When John F. Kennedy was
elected President in 1960, less than 5 per cent of the American people considered themselves outside the religious fold.

It was during this time of tremendous growth that the
churches fancied it necessary to make the faith more "relevant." The effects were nothing short of disastrous. By 1974,
less than 50 per cent of the Catholics in America attended
Mass regularly, while only 37 per cent of the Presbyterians,
32 per cent of the Methodists, and 28 per cent of the
Episcopalians described themselves as steady churchgoers.
Churches have become modern, relevant, and empty. And
each year the decline appears to worsen. Something terrible has happened. The Christian in America, among the
ruins of his religion, knows it. He *feels* it. But it remains
something elusive, something that he can neither locate
nor articulate. Let us try to identify it.

To begin with, we must acknowledge that religion has
played more of a sociological than a religious role in America throughout the twentieth century. Its major function,
in other words, has not been to bring one into the presence
of a transcendent God, but rather to confer a sense of self-
identity within the bewildering complexity of American
society. This, as Will Herberg points out in his classic study
Protestant–Catholic–Jew, was the inevitable result of the
continual waves of immigration that began shortly after the
Civil War. Each year the immigrants came—sometimes at the
rate of 15,000 a day—making America a nation of strangers.

By the end of World War I, 35 million Europeans—the wretched refuse of those teeming shores—had left everything behind to start a new life in the New World. And upon landing, they were lost.

The conditions of American life, Herberg tells us, confronted the immigrant with a problem he had never faced before—the problem of self-identity. A man must be able to identify himself with and among his fellow men, to locate himself in society. But upon reaching the brave new world, the immigrant found that he didn't belong. He became aware that to be an American meant to be an Anglo-Saxon. And, for the most part, the immigrant by his very appearance did not fit into the American mold. He could not identify with America's language, its manners, its way of life. So he sought out those who shared his foreignness. . . .

The immigrants swarmed together in the same sections of the rising cities. They opened their own markets and shops to cater to their own people. They published their own newspapers in their native language. And they also transplanted their own churches. In most cases, these churches became the centers of ethnic life. . . .

But this means of self-identification did not bind the children of the immigrants. The moment they entered school—the moment they went out to play with other children—they were made aware of their difference. Their foreignness became the object of ridicule. . . . And so these children came to look upon their ethnic group as an enslaving force—as a force that prevented their assimilation into American society. Above all, they wished to be transformed and transfigured into "real" Americans like Thomas Jefferson, Abraham Lincoln, and Tom Mix. Thus was the age of Clairol born. Hair was straightened and colored to aid in the assimilation process. At times even features—especially noses—were altered. Dominick Garonski became Don Gordon; Giovanni Pizzo became John Price. Yet, despite these frantic efforts, they were still not "Americans." The men of the second generation remained men of two worlds and strangers in both. The mythical melting pot could not melt them. It could only mask them. And it was frightfully easy to see through the mask.

During this transitional time, the ties to the Old World loosened. The ethnic clubs began to close their doors. Foreign-language newspapers dwindled in scope and circulation. In time, every feature of immigrant life appeared to disintegrate within the new democracy. Everything, that is, except the church. It remained the only link with the past. It alone remained to tell the third generation who they were and where they came from. They were no longer looked upon as foreigners; by their speech, their appearance, their way of life, they were Americans. But what kind of Americans? They needed a qualifier to describe their identity. They needed a sense of belonging to a carefully defined group. . . . And so, by the 1950s, religion became the primary means of self-identification in American society. If someone were asked what he was, his answer would be the brand name of his belief: Protestant, Catholic, or Jew. . . .

Thus it came to pass that religion formed the American people into separate, identifiable clusters. It provided them with a class, a genus, a family group. For this reason, an Irish Catholic felt closer to a Polish Catholic than to a Polish Protestant. They shared a common identity. They possessed the same basic beliefs, the same sacramental *rites de passage,* the same rituals. In the same manner, a lowly Baptist felt more brotherly affection for a lofty Congregationalist than for a Roman Catholic. He saw a Congregationalist as being of the same stuff as he was, while he viewed a Catholic as one of a different breed.

Therefore, even though ethnic endogamy declined, religious endogamy persisted. At the turn of the century, virtually 100 per cent of Poles married Poles, 87 per cent of Germans married Germans, and 75 per cent of Irish married Irish. By the 1950s, less than 50 per cent of Poles, 40 per cent of Irish, and 27 per cent of Germans wedded members of the same ethnic stock. Yet the religious lines remained firm and impassable: more than 85 per cent of

Catholics married Catholics, and 80 per cent of Protestants married Protestants. Intermarriage, for the most part, was looked upon with abhorrence.

In the eyes of her family, a Catholic girl who married a Protestant boy married an outsider. For a Protestant, the idea that his child would be raised as a Catholic meant that his child would never really be *his*. His offspring would be severed from his heritage, from his social group, from himself. He, as a Protestant, would remain a stranger to his own flesh and blood.

Quite naturally, therefore, the Fifties were a time of rigid separatism. Protestant clubs and societies carefully kept their members from contact with Catholics, and vice versa. Private resorts, developments, lake, and country clubs maintained religious restrictions to prevent the invasion of strangers. Rarely did anyone object to these restrictions. People innately understood the sociological importance of separatism. It was the American way of life.

Then came ecumenism in the garb of "enlightenment." It was not the laity but the influential theologians and clerics, both Catholic and Protestant, who fancied it a splendid idea. To these Don Quixotes, intoxicated with the impossible dream of a universal church, separatism was a manifestation of sinfulness and stupidity. It was a barrier to brotherhood that had to be removed at all costs. The Catholic Church, imbued with this new spirit, decided to "open the windows." The Decree on Ecumenicity of the Second Vatican Council reflected this new desire for reconciliation and religio-cultural rapprochement. In line with this decree, conferences between Protestants and Catholics proliferated. A new age had dawned: the age of *aggiornamento*.

Aggiornamento, the key word of Vatican II, means updating, making relevant, replacing the old with the new. This process was facilitated by the use of a new and mundane vernacular liturgy. The translation of the Mass from sacred Latin to secular English had drastic consequences; indeed, the elimination of Latin from the Mass struck a

blow at the very nature of Catholicism. It was Latin that
transcended nationalism and testified to the universality of
the Church. It was Latin that gave the Mass its mystique.
It was Latin that made the Church a *"mysticum corpus"*
[mystical body]. It was Latin that enabled Catholics to
believe they belonged to a strange and mysterious society in
which wondrous words were spoken, words meaningful only
to its members. And it was Latin that sharply distinguished
the Roman rite from Protestant services, and the Catholic
from the non-Catholic, just as a foreign language distinguished the immigrant from other Americans. The removal
of Latin from the Roman rite affected Protestants as well
as Catholics. How could Protestants stress *their* separatism,
preserve *their* uniqueness, now that they spoke the same
language as Catholics?

With the loss of Latin came other changes—minor, to
be sure, but disturbing nevertheless. Until the early Sixties,
Catholics were told it was a mortal sin to participate in
Protestant services. But suddenly priests themselves—even
bishops—began to take an active part in Protestant services
to illustrate the new enlightenment. It finally reached the
point where some nuns, hungry for novelty, actually delivered sermons to several startled Protestant congregations.

Other changes followed. Confused Catholics were in-
structed to sing such Protestant hymns as "Faith of Our
Fathers" and "A Mighty Fortress Is Our God" during Mass.
Litanies and rosaries were replaced by lovebeads and topical
homilies. All reverence for tradition was forgotten in the
consuming quest for relevance. The holy mystery of the
Mass was reduced to the hootenannies of the early Sixties.

The Catholic realized that something was radically
wrong with his world. But what was it? It was something
more significant than the changes in ritual, the removal of
the altar rail and the statues, or the sudden appearance of
nuns in short skirts. It was something that he couldn't voice
—or didn't dare voice. After all, how could he attack the
exalted ideals of ecumenism in the name of Christ? How
could he defend separatism in the name of the sacred? How

could he reject for religion's sake the notions of brotherhood, of sharing with his fellow Christians?

The recalcitrant Catholic could only finger his rosary in
spite. He could but dimly understand that what so dis-
turbed him was nothing less than the Church's turning from
its own to others.

By this turning, the Church abrogated its sociological
role. Most Americans, as we have seen, did not go to church
simply because they were devout. Rather, they went because
it was their means of assuring their self-identity, of confirm-
ing their place within a particular group. They were Catholics or Protestants. This was *what* they were, *who* they were.
Their religion was their roots. And the Church, in turn,
constantly told Catholics that their roots were firm. It stood
as the Rock in a world of chaotic change. It maintained
that its teachings were *semper eadem*—eternal and im-
mutable—binding the generations, bestowing upon Catholics a clearly discernible character, a fixed morality that
reinforced their distinctiveness. The very prayers of the Mass
were punctuated by the phrase *per omnia saecula saecu-
lorum* [through all the ages]. The Protestants, for their part,
stood firm in their opposition to these teachings. In this
way, the Rock was also their Rock; it confirmed their
solidarity in separatism. Then the Rock moved. The ecumenical movement inadvertently shook the earth. Sunday
morning became Saturday night. Flesh replaced fish. The
changeless changed. *Semper* became sometimes. The time-
less itself was temporalized.

It was this sudden shift from separatism that severed
the American people from their roots. Symbolically, Catholics were stripped of their "dogtags"—their St. Christopher
medals—which had proclaimed their identity to the world.
This loss was the price of the desired at-one-ment. Protestants and Catholics now shared the same sacred supper.
"We're all the same anyhow," they were told; "we're all
brothers in Christ."

With the loss of self-identity came a loss of moral character. Under the impact of Vatican II, the fixed moral

teachings of the Church began to waver. By 1963, 40 per cent of American Catholics approved of artificial contraception; ten years later, 83 per cent approved of it. In 1963, less than 12 per cent of Catholics thought that it was not a mortal sin for an engaged couple to have sexual relations; ten years later, 73 per cent held this view. The Catholic character was no longer sharply defined. By 1975, 73 per cent of Catholics approved of remarriage after divorce, and 70 per cent maintained that abortion should be made legal for married women. The changing Church had changed them.

And betrayed them. They had been assured that the Church was changeless—an institution unmoved by the "whips and scorns of time." But Vatican II proved otherwise. Catholics had been deceived. Their roots had not been planted in firm ground. The absolute had become relative. There was no Rock for them to cling to or for Protestants to take a sighting from. American Christians no longer knew their names.

VIEWS OF CATHOLICISM TODAY: II [5]

Mr. Paul Williams has . . . [in the preceding article] delivered himself of a strange set of assertions. His essay . . . seems to promise an inquiry into why faith in Christ is apparently declining in the United States. By the time it ends, however, we have waded through several sociological paragraphs interspersed with liturgical misrepresentations, and only a hint of authentic theology. He leaves the reader puzzling over which upsets him more: the erosion of Christianity (a) as an American's only effective clue to his sociological niche or (b) as a religion.

Mr. Williams' initial lament for the . . . [Latin] liturgy gives way to a justifiably distressed look at the dip that polls tell us has occurred in Catholic and Protestant attendance

[5] From "Sociological 'Religion' Versus Christianity," by John J. Lynch, curate, Church of St. Mary Star of the Sea, Bronx, New York. *National Review.* 27:1171–2+. 0. 29, '76. Reprinted by permission of National Review, 150 E. 35th St., New York, NY 10016. (subscription: $19 per year)

at Sunday worship. "Something terrible has happened. The
Christian in America, among the ruins of his religion, knows
it." But he cannot say exactly what "it" is. Mr. Williams
undertakes to enlighten him. . . . I shall attempt a run-
through of Mr. Williams' major solecisms, and then a different estimate of what spawned the genuine evils he de-
plores. . . .

Mr. Williams . . . [alleges] the abolition of incense, the
silencing of bells, and the disappearance of statues, and
he claims that "even the altar has gone. It has been replaced
by a 'common table.' " Concerning the latter, I refer the
reader to Nos. 259–70 of the Roman document on the new
Order of Mass. The section knows nothing of a "common
table"; the words "altar" and "table" occur 21 and six
times respectively. In the rubrics throughout the remainder
of this official ritual book, the altar is regularly called an
altar.

Mr. Williams' statements on Latin challenged me to
seek one adjective to describe them. I failed. Observe: "The
elimination of Latin from the Mass struck a blow at the
very nature of Catholicism." Hence, we gather, the participants in the Last Supper, the members of the Primitive
Church, and the members of the Eastern Rites that remained in communion with Rome were other than "natural" Catholics. "It was Latin that made the Church a
mysticum corpus"; but the New Testament, itself written
in Greek, says that it is a union of believers in the Spirit
with Christ their Head that makes the Church a *mysticum
corpus* (mystical body). "It was Latin," says Mr. Williams,
"that enabled Catholics to believe they belonged to a
strange and mysterious society in which wondrous words
were spoken, words meaningful only to its members." Is he
implying that gnosticism, a secretive tendency vigorously
condemned by the Church, was orthodox after all?

Over and over Mr. Williams lists real or imagined reforms of *nonessential* practices and reacts as if the Church
had begun teaching Arianism [a fourth century heresy] as
gospel truth.

It is very hard to resist concluding that Mr. Williams believes the separatism which he claims religion fostered in America to be a positive virtue. In fact, separatism within the pale of Christianity—the spectacle of Christians teaching a myriad of contradictory doctrines in the name of Christ and looking with contempt on "outsiders"—is a vice. . . .

Thus what Mr. Williams hails as the principal contribution of religion in America stems from a failure on the part of Christianity adequately to fulfill its mission. This emerges, unintentionally it seems, in one of his own key statements; the "major function" of religion in twentieth century America "has not been to bring one into the presence of a transcendent God, but rather to confer a sense of self-identity within the bewildering complexity of American society."

As a consequence, Mr. Williams errs in his attack on ecumenism. Christians who call Christ their Lord and sincerely desire to follow the promptings of the Spirit are obliged to seek healing for the divisions which have tragically obstructed the apostolic mission of the Church in the world. That some Catholics and Protestants have gone overboard in compromising can never undo this basic principle (any more than a political extremist can automatically invalidate the conservative or liberal position he caricatures). I should not even have to point out that there is no contradiction between a Catholic's acceptance of the authoritative teaching office of the Church and his experiencing profound glimpses into divine truth in the thought of members of other denominations. . . .

Cheap Grace

We cannot dispute the fact that the decline of "separatism" has occurred side by side with an apparently widespread abandonment by Christians of Sunday worship and by Catholics of the Church's teachings on sexual morality and abortion. To blame Vatican II for this, however, is as valid as to say that the Church has anathematized statues and altars, or that Latin created the Mystical Body. There are at least two complementary reasons for the present state of Catholicism. One arose as an unnecessary by-product of the atmosphere generated by Pope John and the Council; the other has its roots in what we might term an "admissions-policy" defect of long standing.

Taking the latter first, we find Mr. Williams himself inadvertently hinting at it in his analysis of the role of religion in American life. To say that religion has been for most Americans a matter of belonging to a sociological grouping rather than a means of attaining to God is to announce the reason for the state in which the churches find themselves.

The most telling portrayal of this appears in *The Cost of Discipleship* by German theologian and martyr Dietrich Bonhoeffer—an orthodox Christian despite the statements of a few religious non-experts. Bonhoeffer agonized over the failure of much of his Evangelical (Lutheran) Church to serve as a bulwark against Nazism. He rightly discerned that this failure was traceable to churchmen's emphasis on the routine bestowal of sacraments to the detriment of insistence on personal commitment to Christ and the gospel. He labeled this phenomenon "cheap grace." . . .

The existence of a vast number of "sociological Catholics" and the failure of the Church to do anything consistent and decisive about it—is the fundamental cause of the Church's distress. Once the Council enacted its reforms, which left the essential dogmatic position of the Church intact, numerous nominal Catholics who had been (out of superstition, social pressure, or inertia) going through minimal motions seized on the reforms as an excuse. They joined the already sizable army of those who, save for involuntary *pro forma* childhood sacraments, had not even been bothering with the motions. . . .

Hierarchical Passivity

To repeat, all this began before Vatican II. Moreover, the sacramental reforms—especially the baptismal rites—

which have been issued as a result of the Council make it clear that evangelization and *acceptance* of the gospel are necessary prerequisites for sacraments.

The bishops' conferences of most nations have failed to draw up uniform rules on matters of cheap grace, despite Vatican II's instructing them to do so. Predictably, there are plenty of cheap-grace parishes available to help sociological Catholics rest secure in their ungodly living. Which leads us to the second reason I am adducing for the Church's present condition: the episcopate's frustrating reluctance to exercise its authority in the face of persistent doctrinal, moral, liturgical, sacramental, and canonical aberrations—frequently well publicized. . . .

Very soon, therefore, the episcopate must confront the issues of right belief and right conduct. This will require well-considered, responsible, and firm actions. Such actions will have consequences, conceivably including a measurable shrinkage in the number of "Roman Catholics" on census rolls. . . .

Effective moves against cheap grace and heterodox teaching—whatever the results—will be essential steps toward re-establishing the episcopate's credibility and authority. And the Church's. This cannot happen too soon.

IV. VARIETIES OF RELIGIOUS EXPERIENCE

EDITOR'S INTRODUCTION

This section discusses a number of diverse religious experiences, each directly concerned with a significant, though relatively small, segment of the population.

The first selection reviews the challenges facing Judaism in the United States today; the second surveys a faith of rapidly expanding influence—the Church of Jesus Christ of Latter-Day Saints, popularly called the Mormons.

The next two selections concern black Americans. Blacks are little different from their white counterparts in seeking and following a wide range of religions. There are, however, important sects that are predominantly or exclusively black. Two of these are examined here: the African Methodist Episcopal Zion Church, with its history of devotion to freedom and the pursuit of civil rights; and the Nation of Islam, a community emphasizing a separatist society for its members.

The next article, by George E. La More, Jr., examines Transcendental Meditation. Asian in origin, TM is followed by many who also claim some other religious faith and provides a psychological as well as a spiritual experience for its participants. (Other Eastern religions, taken up enthusiastically by some young Americans in recent years, are discussed in Section V.)

The belief known as atheism—the denial of the existence of God or gods and of any supernatural power—is examined in a New York *Times Magazine* article that reports on the Society of Separationists, a leading atheist organization.

This section next takes up the subject of women as spiritual leaders. In the congregations of some American sects, women in the pulpit are not unknown; but this has not been the case in Catholicism, the Conservative and Orthodox branches of Judaism, and a number of Protestant churches. The selection included here reports on the ordination of the first women priests in the Episcopal Church—an inflammatory issue that has led traditionalists to disassociate themselves from the church leadership that approved the action.

The final selection, by *Christian Century* editor Martin E. Marty, discusses the attitudes of religious bodies toward the proposed Equal Rights Amendment to the United States Constitution.

NEW CHALLENGES FOR JUDAISM [1]

Reprinted from *U.S. News & World Report.*

A haunting question is arising in the ranks of U.S. Jews: Can their ancient faith, in the years ahead, survive the success that has come their way?

For nearly 1,000 years, Judaism flourished in countless ghettos of the West where it was an inner resource that helped Jews to survive restrictive laws and persecution.

Today, all that has changed in this country.

In attaining influence and affluence in the mainstream of American society, the nation's 6 million Jews have left the urban enclaves of their parents and grandparents and moved to suburbia and exurbia. Many have assimilated and shed their religious identities.

Now, the freedom that enabled Jews to succeed in America is seen as a threat to the survival of their religion. Says Rabbi Alexander M. Schindler, president of the Union of American Hebrew Congregations: "Our biggest problem is that we live in a land of freedom. No one would exchange it for the ghetto. But freedom means social mixing; freedom means intermarriage. For too many, freedom means breaking away."

Some leaders point to statistics on intermarriage and

[1] "Judaism: An Ancient Faith Looks to a New Kind of Challenge." *U.S. News & World Report.* 82:68–9. Ap. 11, '77.

membership in synagogues as evidence of the crisis they see confronting Judaism.

The intermarriage rate of Jews is climbing rapidly. With assimilation have come mixed marriages. Between 1960 and 1972, the intermarriage rate jumped from 5.9 per cent to 31.7 per cent. Some leaders now put it at close to 40 per cent.

Infrequent Attendance

As for the synagogue, less than half of the heads of Jewish households belong to congregations, and most Jews do not attend with any frequency.

But in mapping strategy for a renaissance of Judaism—especially among the young—Jewish scholars point out this: Disturbing as the figures appear, there is another—less gloomy—way of looking at them.

In spite of the growing rate of intermarriage, most of the children of mixed marriages are brought up as members of the Jewish faith.

A study of intermarriage by the Council of Jewish Federations and Welfare Funds found that where the wife is Jewish, 98.4 per cent of the children are raised as Jews. Where the husband is Jewish, the figure drops, but it is still a relatively high 63.3 per cent.

In addition, almost half of non-Jewish spouses come to regard themselves as Jewish, even though many of them do not formally convert.

Synagogue figures are deceptive, too. Traditionally, Jews in the United States have not attended synagogues in large numbers. Biggest attendance comes on the High Holy Days rather than on the Sabbath.

Unlike Christianity, Judaism is a culture as well as a religion—making it possible for Jews to maintain their heritage, yet not take an active role in synagogue life.

Says Rabbi Marc Tanenbaum, national director of interreligious affairs of the American Jewish Committee: "Jews may not identify with a synagogue, but the institutions in which they express their peoplehood remain a vital force."

Series of Circles

Daniel J. Elazar, a political scientist at Temple University, sees the Jewish community as a series of concentric circles radiating outward from a small, but committed, "hard core" toward "gray areas of semi-Jewishness," where a majority consider themselves Jewish, but participate in Jewish activities only to a limited extent.

Elazar believes that there is considerable fluidity among those circles, with Jews moving back and forth according to circumstances.

One circumstance that has caused many Jews to move closer—for a time—to the center circle is the continuing threat to Israel's survival. Though many U.S. Jews do not regard Israel as their homeland, they see that nation as the embodiment of their heritage. Its survival is a unifying force among American Jewry. . . .

Rich Mixture

This new interest in Israel was taking place at the same time that ethnic pluralism was gaining respectability in the United States. The image of America as a melting pot was giving way to America as beef stew, a rich mixture of many ingredients. Assimilation and conformity were no longer the order of the day.

Some young Jews, reacting against their parents' assimilation, began to take a deep interest in their heritage.

But others, for a variety of reasons, joined the counterculture or opted for sects such as Jews for Jesus. An American Jewish Committee study estimates that 10 to 15 per cent of Jewish youth were part of the counterculture.

This caused Jewish leaders to do some soul searching. A special effort was made to instill a sense of history in young Jews by stressing the Holocaust suffered at the hands of the Nazis.

But Rabbi Harold Schulweis, leader of a congregation in Encino, Calif., believes that reaching into the past was not enough. He says: "I think it's important to try to teach people to remember. But you can't scare Jews into being Jews."

Leaders sought a more individual, less institutional, approach to give Judaism meaning for the young. This led to the formation of *havurah* or fellowship.

A *havurah* consists of clusters of people who come together to educate each other about their religion and to share joy and sorrow. It is the modern equivalent of the extended family.

Both Jewish leaders and young people who returned to Judaism from the counterculture were instrumental in the developing *havurot* that have parallels with communes. . . .

Not all *havurot* are *avant-garde*. Rabbi Schulweis helped to establish *havurot* in his congregation. He sees the groups as "a substitute for the survival pressure that used to keep the Jewish people together, but which no longer exists in modern society."

Maintaining Identity

With Jews more mobile and dispersing to regions few Jews live in, *havurah* provides a way for individuals to maintain their Jewish identity. It takes the place of the close-knit Jewish families of past generations.

The *havurah* movement is one of several signs that Judaism maintains vitality despite assimilation. Some others:

☐ College programs in Jewish studies are on the upsurge. In the past 20 years, between 75 and 100 schools have developed majors in Jewish studies.

☐ Enrollment in full-time Jewish day schools is on the rise. It climbed from 60,000 in 1966 to 82,000 last year.

☐ The number of synagogues which have expanded their schedules at religious schools from one to several days a week has jumped 50 per cent in the last few years.

☐ Since 1966, the average number of hours that youngsters spend annually in religious schools has climbed from 182 to 248.

☐ Thirty-two new congregations are being formed annually

by the Reform branch of Judaism after a decade in which an average of five branches a year were added.

☐ *The Jewish Catalog,* a book that fuses the counter-culture with Jewish tradition and learning, has sold 180,000 copies since it was first published in 1973. A second volume, with a printing of 60,000, has just come out.

Reasons for Worrying

With these signs of health, why are so many Jewish leaders worried about the future?

Some fear that the positive trends are not strong enough to counteract assimilation and intermarriage. They also worry about the Jewish birth rate, which is the lowest of the major religions and may well be below zero-population growth.

They are concerned about what Yehuda Rosenman, director of the Jewish communal-affairs department of the American Jewish Committee, calls "the passive erosion of the practice of Judaism." That is, Jews continue to identify themselves as members of the faith, but they no longer take an active part in religious activities.

Brandeis University sociologist Marshall Sklare sees these developments as leading to a smaller Jewish community in the future.

But, he says, that community will be "more vital" because even while some Jews are becoming less active, others are intensifying their participation in Jewish community life.

Sklare's Brandeis colleague, Bernard Reisman, professor of American Jewish communal studies, puts down those who see a gloomy future. Says Reisman: "There is a tendency in Jewish life to sustain crises. Jews can't get comfortable with success."

CHURCH IN THE NEWS: STORY OF
MORMON SUCCESS [2]

Reprinted from *U.S. News & World Report.*

It is a faith unique among the world's religions, the Church of Jesus Christ of Latter-Day Saints—the Mormons—that is claiming much attention at this time. . . .

Only a quarter of a century ago, this Church had about 860,000 members. Most of them were to be found in Utah and in nearby Arizona, Idaho and southern California.

Today Mormon missionaries scour the globe, adding thousands of converts each month. Membership, worldwide, now comes to about 2.4 million.

A Way of Life

It is in this Western "homeland" of the Church [Salt Lake City], however, that you get the most complete look at what is not only a religion but a closely bound society.

A Mormon family in good standing is likely to spend three or four evenings a week working for the Church—in Bible studies, visiting the sick, converting the non-Mormons, or supervising a Church-run troop of Boy Scouts, for instance. Such work would be in addition to auxiliary duties in the Women's Relief Society and similar groups.

Mormon adults are expected to give one tenth of their income to the Church, and entire families are called upon to fast for two meals each month—donating to the Church's vast program of welfare the money that would have been spent on those meals.

"Ours is not an easy religion," one high official of the Church said. "We expect it to govern the individual's total life."

In Salt Lake City, a Mormon is likely to get his news from the Church-owned daily. He can watch network television on a Church-owned station.

Downtown, he may work in a new office building put

[2] From "Church in the News: Story of Mormon Success." *U.S. News & World Report.* 61:90–2+. S. 26, '66.

up by the Church, park his car in a Church-owned garage and go to work in the city's biggest hotel, also owned by the Church. The member's home may have been financed through a bank owned in part by the Church. And his insurance may be carried by a Church-owned corporation.

Furthermore, his wife is likely to do an important share of her shopping at one of two department stores owned by the Zion's Co-operative Mercantile Institution. And their son or daughter may be a student in Provo, Utah, at Brigham Young University, the largest Church-operated school in the nation.

Nor does the Church's impact end there.

If hard times befall the "Saint," he can get food, clothing, medicine and necessary cash through the Church's own "welfare state." He is required to work for this help to the limit of his physical ability, and a lazy Mormon may be sent to a psychiatrist, at the expense of the Church, to find out what is wrong with him.

One measure of the Church's scope here: It occupies more than two full pages in the Salt Lake City telephone directory—as against less than a page for the State offices.

"Conservative" Viewpoint

What emerges is a Church that stirs criticism as well as admiration among Utah's non-Mormon or "gentile" minority. Some describe the Church as being "totalitarian" and its members as "zealots."

Among some Mormons as well as outsiders there is discussion of a doctrine under which Negroes can join the Church but are not eligible for the priesthood. . . .

Controversy also is being heard over a rather "conservative" viewpoint on political and social issues that seems to prevail among members of this Church.

Some Backsliders

Many Mormons, themselves, find the Church's demands too rigorous and have become nominal members—or "Jack

Mormons," a term applied originally to friendly outsiders.

Such Mormons no longer attend Church or do so irregularly. They might smoke or drink alcohol or tea—all forbidden to Mormons in good standing. But they are regarded, and continue to regard themselves, as Mormons, unless they request excommunication—or are excommunicated by the hierarchy for actions deemed hostile to the Church. That action probably is taken against no more than a handful of persons year by year.

Dropouts are far outnumbered by the 90,000 or more who are converted annually to Mormonism. And best estimates are that most Mormons practice their religion faithfully. One of the practicing Mormons explained:

"To become even a 'Jack Mormon' would require a total reorganization of your life, even your social life. Just to fill up three or four evenings a week would be a big job, and you would have to develop a whole new circle of friends and work out an entirely new set of interests."

How It Started

Mormonism has its roots in the early 1800s, when Americans were caught up not only in religious revivalism but in utopian experiments such as Brook Farm, in which "communal living" played a strong role.

It was in 1830 that Joseph Smith, a young man in upstate New York, published *The Book of Mormon*, which he described as a translation from ancient plates buried nearby but given to him temporarily by an angel named Moroni. This volume relates the narrative of a Jewish migration to the Americas about 600 B.C.

Mormons believe that one group of these migrants, remained faithful to its heritage, was visited by—and converted to—the resurrected Christ. The other group, becoming apostate, eventually formed the basis of Indian tribes.

The Book of Mormon says that the Christian group was annihilated by the apostates in a great battle that took place about 440 A.D. in the eastern part of North America. A prophet named Mormon and his son, Moroni, the narra-

tive says, preserved ancient records on the plates that were
later given to Joseph Smith.

Today, Mormons proclaim the literal truth of the Bible
and the divinity of Christ. But several beliefs set them apart
from "Protestant" Christianity. Among them are these:

☐ In Mormon homes, *The Book of Mormon* occupies a place alongside the Bible as the Word of God. Two
other books are regarded as divinely inspired. One is *The
Book of Doctrine and Covenants,* a compilation of revela-
tions held given to the Church by God through Joseph
Smith and subsequent prophets. The other, *The Pearl of
Great Price,* contains what are described as missing pieces
of Old Testament scripture which Smith said he translated
from papyri found in an Egyptian tomb.

☐ The Church of Jesus Christ of Latter-Day Saints
holds itself to be the true or "restored" Church—not a
Protestant denomination.

☐ The general run of Mormon meeting places is open
to all. But only "Saints" in good standing are permitted
to enter a Temple, of which there are 13 in the world, to
participate in the most sacred ceremonies of the Church.

So "different" was this religion, steeped in early-Ameri-
can utopianism as well as Old Testament zeal, that Mormons became one of the most persecuted sects in the nation's history—driven by angry "gentiles" from one place to
another.

In 1844, Joseph Smith and his brother Hyrum were
killed by a mob in Carthage, Ill. And two years later, several thousand "Saints" began a march westward to a new
"homeland" in a remote and arid region unwanted by other
pioneers en route to Oregon or California.

Epic Journey

That trek, organized and led by Brigham Young, the
successor to Joseph Smith, is described by historians as one
of the great epics of U.S. history.

Mormons by the hundreds died from disease, exposure

or starvation. Some families literally walked the 1,300 miles to the new settlement near the Great Salt Lake, pulling and pushing two-wheeled handcarts. Of these men, women and children, one sixth died.

Even in those times, many visitors were impressed by the collective zeal and discipline of the Mormon pioneers in building irrigation works and tilling the soil of an unpromising frontier to make it "bloom like a rose."

Within a few years after starting their settlement in Salt Lake Valley, Mormons were building villages throughout the West as far as 500 miles away. By 1857, these settlements came to 135, with a population of about 76,000 persons, in California, Idaho, Wyoming, Arizona and New Mexico.

Today Mormons are an especially potent force in Idaho, where they have by far the largest membership of any single church, and in Arizona. In much of the West, it is common for travelers to find not only a "Gideon" Bible, but the *Book of Mormon* in their hotel rooms. [The Gideons, a Christian society of commercial travelers, place Bibles in hotel rooms.—Ed.]

The Church, in its early days, found itself in deep trouble with the U.S. Government, which, by court action, took control of the Church corporation and held its property for several years. Within the Church itself, schisms and quarrels threatened its unity.

What brought about this crisis was mainly the doctrine of polygamy, described by Smith as a "revelation" from God. Until outlawed by the hierarchy in 1890, it brought the Church into virtually open warfare with the U.S. Government. Today, some of the "splinter" sects that have broken off from the Church still believe in polygamy. Thousands of persons are said to practice it in Utah and Arizona, as well as Mexico. Such persons, upon discovery, face excommunication by the Church.

Out of that crisis survived a Church that some theologians have called "Judaism Within Christianity," bearing a strong flavor of Old Testament simplicity and zeal.

But the Church is rooted, too, in Puritan ideals of hard

work, respect for law, individual responsibility and the idea of communal welfare.

A Year's Food Supply

Dozens of small towns scattered over Utah, southern Idaho and northern Arizona are largely Mormon—and different.

As one example:

Heber City, about 40 miles southeast of Salt Lake City, has about 5,000 persons in town and countryside. Only 240 are non-Mormons.

All but about 50 families in this community own their homes. Most adhere to Mormon doctrine that each family should keep a year's supply of canned food on hand for emergency use.

Heber City has a police department of four men—kept busy mostly on traffic violations, with occasional complaints about barking dogs to investigate.

Doors Unguarded

A little more than a year ago townspeople were somewhat surprised when police reported a case of "breaking and entering." Even today, however, householders are rather casual about locking their houses or cars. Mayor Albert Winterrose said:

"I guess it is peaceful here, or dull, depending on how you look at it."

Most youngsters take part in one or another of many youth activities run by Mormons—theater, sports, dancing and Scouting. The high-school graduating class of 1966, over a four-year period, lost only 16 out of 132 students. And more than half the graduates are going on to college.

Except for a Catholic priest who visits the town weekly, there is no "gentile" religious activity. However, non-Mormons are to be found in Boy Scout troops and some even attend Church socials.

Looking at the impact of Mormonism on a broader

scale, Henry Pearson, director of the Utah Foundation, a nonprofit research agency specializing on governmental spending and economics, made this comment: "Not only public policies in Utah, but the entire economy and social outlook reflect the ideals of the early Mormon pioneers."

State spending, on a "pay as you go" basis, is geared to Mormon principles of thrift. Property-tax rates are well below the national average.

In the decade that ended in 1963, while the national average of State and local spending on relief was rising by 40 per cent, Utah reduced such spending by 25 per cent. Utah's per capita expenditure in 1963 was $6.83, less than two thirds of the national average.

Spending on schools, by contrast, is high—based on Mormon belief that "the glory of God is intelligence." Utah leads all other States in the proportion of young people who graduate from high school, enroll in college or pursue scientific careers.

Employers generally rate the State high on industrial productivity and low on absenteeism. An electronics firm reported that its Utah plant, with an eighth of the corporation's employees, turns out one fifth of its production.

Utah's crime rate is well below the national average. . . .

No Paid Clergy

This impact on the community comes from a Church that has no professional clergy.

All males, except Negroes, are eligible for the priesthood on reaching the age of 12. Altogether, 600,000 men serve— some in the "Melchizedek" or higher priesthood, others in the "Aaronic" or lower order, usually composed of youths.

Each local congregation or "ward," consisting of as many as 500 persons, is administered by a bishop and two counselors. Several such congregations, as many as 10, constitute a "stake," supervised by a president and two counselors. A Church official said:

"We see to it that everyone gets involved, or has the

opportunity of getting involved, in Church and community work. When a congregation reaches a certain size, we divide it into two 'wards.' This doubles the number of officers, therefore doubles the opportunity for service."

At the top level of the worldwide Church are the "general authorities."

Chief of these is the President, who also holds the title of Prophet, and serves until his death. . . .

Assisting the President are four counselors, and 12 Apostles who, among other duties, pick the President from their ranks—usually the senior Apostle in length of service.

Below these leaders are 23 other officers in the top hierarchy. Together, they administer 6,000 congregations, 12,000 full-time missionaries in 51 countries, 3 universities and colleges, 190 religious institutes that serve Mormon students in college, 2,000 seminaries for public-school students, and 15 hospitals.

Welfare for All

As remarkable as any of its other services is the Church's welfare program, which reaches 100,000 Mormons at an estimated cost of 10 million dollars, or more, annually.

Through the Women's Relief Society, the bishop of each "ward" learns of families in need of help. These persons then can go to one of the nearest "bishop's storehouses," of which there are about 100, with a "bishop's order" for help that can be given over the counter.

Every day, into such "storehouses" flows a steady stream of food, clothing and other articles for the poor. Some of it comes from Mormon-owned enterprises such as canneries and clothing factories. But much, if not most, comes from the hard labor of ordinary Mormons everywhere.

Church members contribute by gathering fruit and vegetables in the fields, and taking them to a processing plant to do the canning themselves—lawyers and businessmen working alongside their wives.

If you visit the biggest "storehouse," located at Welfare

Square in Salt Lake City, you find on its shelves toothpaste made by Mormons in New York, gelatin manufactured by laymen in Kansas City, Mo., peanut butter churned by members of the Houston "stake," and grapefruit juice canned by the "Saints" in Arizona—and many other articles made and contributed by Mormons across the U.S.

Jobs for Needy

Thousands of needy persons—the blind, the crippled, the elderly and retarded—are at work in "storehouses" and other Church-run projects.

An official of the Church's welfare program said: "We find it boosts their morale to feel they are contributing something—that they're not paupers."

Years ago, in the "New Deal" era, the Church made it an aim of its welfare program that "the curse of idleness would be done away with, the evils of a dole abolished, and independence, industry, thrift and self-respect once more established amongst our people."

This statement continued:

"The aim of the Church is to help the people to help themselves. Work is to be re-enthroned as the ruling principle of the lives of our Church membership."

Such a viewpoint is seen by many as tending to align the Church on the side of "conservative" politicians. . . .

Federal Aid Rejected

Mormon-run institutions reject any form of federal handout. Ernest Wilkinson, the president of Brigham Young University, pointed out that this school carried through a building program costing 60 million dollars without accepting any offers of federal grants.

. . . In 1965 the President and Prophet, [David O.] McKay, wrote the 11 Mormons in Congress prior to the vote on repeal of "right to work" laws, voicing his hope that Congress would not abrogate "the God-given rights of men to exercise free agency in seeking and maintaining work privileges."

The picture of the Church as being rigidly "conservative," however, is becoming less clear than it might have been at one time.

Seven of the 11 Mormons in Congress voted for repeal of "right to work" laws. . . .

Some intellectuals, however, are voicing discontent with the pace of change. An educator said:

"Considering its Biblical literalism, the Church does remarkably well in accommodating its intellectuals, especially in the sciences. And it in no way undertakes to give orders to the University of Utah. But it doesn't encourage intellectual activity. It is highly intellectualistic and verbal, but it is not freely speculative—Mormons think about their theology within clearly defined lines. Today's leadership is far more circumscribed in its thinking than Joseph Smith was."

As one step toward meeting dissatisfaction with Church rigidity, some Mormon thinkers . . . started a magazine called *Dialogue*. While independent of Church control, its first issue—in the words of one reader—was "nothing to stir up anybody's blood pressure."

Non-Mormon Views

Among "gentiles," some anti-Mormon feeling is still evident here. One outsider put it this way:

"You can't get to know them through social means, because they're so darned busy with the Church. And they tend to prefer each other in business, too, though maybe not as much as before."

Mormons' missionary zeal also stirs resistance among "gentiles" and "Jack Mormons." One woman who stopped going to church years ago said: "It took them years to give up on me, really. Every week or so there would be the regular caller, brightly smiling, and ready to talk for hours to show me how groundless my doubts were. But the truth was, I couldn't take any more of that incessant work for the Church—it was almost as if the idea was to keep you so busy you wouldn't have time to stop and ask any questions."

Spreading the Faith

Yet the Church keeps growing.

Each year, a new crop of 6,000 young men and women go out to posts elsewhere in the U.S., or abroad, to serve two-year terms as unpaid, full-time missionaries. From the Church, they get money only for transportation to and from their posts. Daily living costs are borne by themselves or their families—often at great hardship.

Even this corps of dedicated missionaries, however, is held by most observers to be only a partial answer to the secret of Mormon growth in recent years.

Dr. Sterling McMurrin, a Mormon who is also professor of philosophy at the University of Utah and formerly U.S. Commissioner of Education, said:

"It seems to me that the convert is likely to be a Bible-oriented person . . . attracted to what you might call the totally 'integrated' life of the devout Mormon. In Mormonism he finds a home that makes it easier for him to withstand pressures of modern society, because it eliminates the conflicts between religious ideals and daily living."

Shifting Conditions

Mormons concede that conditions are changing for the Church. Complaints are heard about the growing number of Mormons getting welfare checks from government—and . . . [the] Church headquarters here was picketed by a woman protesting Mormon doctrine on Negroes. At Brigham Young University, a citadel of the faith, Mr. Wilkinson said:

"It used to be our tradition that teachers were glad to serve their Church and students without worrying about salary schedules.

"Now they're bargaining for higher pay just like teachers elsewhere."

Today, with the Church showing more gains in membership and prestige than at any time in its often-stormy past, one Church member summed up its problems this way:

"In the past we were able to survive persecution and adversity. Now it is success that we must survive."

THE AFRICAN METHODIST EPISCOPAL ZION CHURCH [3]

At the end of the order of worship each Sunday at Martin Temple AME Zion Church on Chicago's South Side, red-and-white-robed members of the choir descend from behind the sanctuary singing a joyful recessional. They are followed by two altar boys and their pastor, Rev. Nathaniel Jarrett Jr., whose salt and pepper hair lends authority to his tall, youthful bearing. He marches slowly down the center aisle and with a poetic cadence asks a benediction for the members of his small congregation. "As you leave this house of God," he prays, "and go but to toil in the fields of your daily endeavors, may the Lord give you strength against adversity and protection against all harm."

Rev. Jarrett's benediction and inspirational message is an almost ritualistic recitation that has fallen on the ears of black people since their earliest association—while in slavery—with Christianity in America. In many ways Christianity represented a contradiction: on the one hand it was a promise for justice, while on the other it was used to maintain blacks in bondage. But throughout the history of the black church—a history formed and shaped to a large degree by the AME Zion Church—Sunday service and benediction has been a source of motivation, courage, strength and leadership against an army of oppressors.

The more than one million members of the African Methodist Episcopal Zion Church are fond of calling their

[3] From "The Ship of AME Zion Rides a Freedom Tide," by Martin Weston, former staff writer. Ebony. 32:75–6+. N. '76. Reprinted by permission of Ebony Magazine, copyright, 1976 by Johnson Publishing Company, Inc.

black Methodist denomination "the freedom church." They point, with unabashed pride, to the strong, effective anti-slavery voices that rose from Zion before the Great Emancipation. Zion, they will tell you, is the church of Frederick Douglass, Sojourner Truth, Harriet Tubman and Catherine Harris—names high on the honor roll of the abolitionist movement of the 19th century. "Many of them (freedom crusaders and abolitionists) received their impetus and great encouragement from the church," says Zion historian Dr. David Bradley Sr., "and the church no doubt had tremendous influence on these aggressive leaders." . . .

The African Methodist Episcopal Zion Church is one of several religious denominations that evolved from Methodism, John Benjamin Wesley's revival of the Church of England (the Protestant Episcopal Church) in the 18th century. The African designation defines the AME Zion's origin among black freemen and slaves during the early 1800s. Episcopal refers both to the Methodist background of the church and its episcopal form of government, a government by bishops. The final designation, Zion, distinguishes one of two separations by blacks from the Methodist Church in America—the one led by James Varick, an itinerant shoemaker and schoolteacher who was also a gifted preacher in New York City's John Street Methodist Church. The other separation was led by the first black Methodist Bishop, Richard Allen, at Bethel Church in Philadelphia. James Varick is the founder of the AME Zion Church in America, and Richard Allen is the father of the African Methodist Episcopal Church, which shares a kinship with Zion and a parallel development. The differences between the AME Zion Church and the AME Church are more social than the result of strong divergent religious beliefs.

The image of the black slave forever suffering, in low spirits and helplessly awaiting his eventual reward for his present burdensome circumstance is a myth. Some slaves were religiously inclined, to be sure. Others could have cared less. Yet the Methodist message to the largely non-Christian blacks yielded a bountiful response, says Harry

V. Richardson, whose new book, *Dark Salvation,* is an excellent study of the development of Methodism as it spread among blacks in America. In simple language that uneducated men could understand, fervent Methodist preachers reinforced religious blacks' basic belief in the error [of] sin and that ultimately sin stood convicted in the sight of God. But the joyful, transporting experience that Methodist evangelists aroused among blacks was that faith in Christ and the forgiveness of God yields salvation. Salvation was available to everyone; bondage in slavery didn't matter. Religious gospel, however, surrendered to rigid social customs both North and South, and before long black Methodists were sitting in special balconies, standing along the sides or in the back, of "white" churches, or attending separate services conducted by white missionaries.

The obvious resentment was first vented with significant intensity when Richard Allen and two other blacks were virtually pulled from their knees while at prayer at St. George's Church in Philadelphia in 1787. "We all went out in a body," says Allen, "and they were no more plagued with us in the church." With this there was the first move toward setting up a place where black Methodists could worship together without being humiliated. The efforts were successful and eventually Bethel Church in Philadelphia became the first black Methodist church, and by 1816 it had spawned the AME Church as the first great black separate denomination.

Unlike the antagonism and wrangling that characterized the break of the AME Church (Bethel) in Philadelphia, for the most part, the separation of AME Zion was, by most accounts, an amicable development. But deliverance from the womb of the white Methodist Church was for the same reasons, of course: the inability or unwillingness of the mother church to satisfactorily accommodate its black members. Black members of John Street (Methodist) Church in New York met with their bishop concerning the growing number of blacks in the church and the separate meetings which had become customary. Christopher Rush, the first historian of AME Zion, writes that the black members were given permission to meet "in the interval of the regular preaching hours of our white brethren," and were told to conduct their services "in the best manner they could."

These and subsequent events suggest that the birth of Zion "was not a protest meeting," historian David Bradley insists. Black Methodist members met separately with the idea that they could do more evangelizing of blacks if they were not in the white church. They felt they would be more free to express their own brand of the Methodist religion. Indeed, the articles incorporating the AME Zion Church, drawn up in 1784, "were done in a friendly manner as an agreement with the mother church," Bradley says. "The birth of Zion developed from a desire for fellowship among black Methodist worshippers, a communion among black believers, and a development of their own black ministry."

From its rather modest beginnings in 1824, AME Zion has experienced steady growth in membership and has become an important force in the total black community. Its appeal is largely due to its doctrine of the inseparable nature of man's wordly concerns and spiritual needs. "The church has to be involved in the total process of life and in the lives of the people it serves," says Bishop Arthur Marshall Jr., a member of the AME Zion Board of Bishops —the body which interprets church law and policy. "It must lift society to the standard of the church as to what constitutes a better way of life."

It is not surprising, therefore, that Zion has been in the forefront of struggles for freedom and justice for all men, and especially its black brethren. "The black church is the most free institution the black man has ever had," says Bishop George J. Leake. "It has been a catalyst in the civil rights movement; it has provided mutual burial societies; organizational structures for the black community; and educational structures for the black community; and educational institutions." Zion is a traditional black community pillar of strength in times of adversity. "Black Zionists were organizing schools for black youngsters while they could still hear the sound of Confederate cannon," says Bishop Alfred Dunston Jr.

And in the 1970s it faces new challenges, says Bishop Marshall. . . . "There are hard issues we must confront like homosexuality, abortion and family planning. We cannot evade them, not anymore." Bishop Marshall teaches that "the individual is of inscrutable worth in the sight of God and according to the scriptures salvation must be offered to him at all cost. We cannot condone homosexuality as a practice however (I'm not so sure it is a sickness) because we believe in the concept of sex for the procreation of the race."

There are other modern concerns, like birth control. "Personally I believe it is for the preservation of the family —the well-being of the family," Bishop Marshall says. "Crowded families deprive the individual of the fullest development of their personality." And on abortion his stand is equally firm, but by no means as liberal as other controversial positions he has assumed: "Life is sacred and must be preserved at all costs," he says.

It is likely that Zion will meet the challenges of the future as it has so many others in the past. Butler Chapel AME Zion Church is where educator Booker T. Washington opened Tuskegee Institute in Alabama and operated the institution for two years before moving it to its own campus. Early in the history of Zion there was felt an urgent need for a collegiate and theological institution for the training of clergy and the advanced education of many of the followers of Zion. From that desire Livingstone College was founded in 1879 in North Carolina. Later Hood Theological Seminary was built. Today the church supports Livingstone and Hood, in addition to Clinton Junior College in Rock Hill, S.C., Lomax-Hannon Junior College in Greenville, Ala., and several other small institutions of higher learning around the country.

Maintaining these institutions requires the kind of commitment that means a bright future for the . . . [more than 1,500 AME Zion churches in America] says senior

Bishop Herbert B. Shaw. "Our church is giving unique leadership to the religious world," he says. "We seek to divest ourselves of all things that are not conducive to the full implementation of ideals brought to the world by Jesus Christ. That means continuing the fight against repression, discrimination or anything that inhibits man from becoming the best that is within him."

THE NATION OF ISLAM [4]

The "Nation of Islam" is perhaps the most successful mass movement of Black people in the United States. Founded 43 years ago in Detroit, Michigan by Elijah Muhammad, it is now a multi-million dollar international operation. It published Black America's largest weekly newspaper and has a network of temples, universities and business enterprises throughout the United States. Since the death of Muhammad a few months ago, the leadership of the movement has passed to his son W. D. Muhammad, who has announced radical changes in its philosophy and membership. In this interview Abdul Haleen Farrakhan, National Representative of W. D. Muhammad, talks to Africa *Assistant Editor, Howard Lee, about the movement's beliefs and aims.*

Africa: Minister Farrakhan, how would you describe the Nation of Islam to an outsider?

Farrakhan: The Nation of Islam is a group of Black brothers and sisters in the United States who have formed themselves into a unit, under the divine guidance of Islam and the Holy Q'uran [Koran] for the purpose of solving the many problems that we face, and have faced, as Black people in White America.

Africa: How would you say the Nation differs from traditional civil rights organizations such as the National Associ-

[4] From "Abdul Farrakhan, minister, Nation of Islam," interview by Howard Lee, assistant editor. *Africa.* No. 50:60—1+. O. '75. Reprinted by permission.

ation for the Advancement of Colored people (NAACP) or
the Urban League?

Farrakhan: The civil rights groups have worked to make
inroads within the system, to frame laws that protect and
guarantee justice for Black people. All of these advances
made by the civil rights movement we admire and applaud.
However, our thrust has been the individual. We are not
looking for outsiders to do for us what we believe we could
unite and do for ourselves. So, while the civil rights groups
might picket to get an inroad into this company or the
other company, or to get more jobs, or to get more rights,
we believe that we have the power within ourselves to
create these right within ourselves.

Africa: What specific things could you point to as evidence of your success in creating an independent or self-
reliant Black economy?

Farrakhan: The first thing that the Honourable Master
Elijah Muhammad (may peace be upon him) taught us
is that we had to go to the earth because we are a nation of
consumers rather than a nation of producers. For us to be
productive, he said, we must have some earth that we can
call our own. So we pooled our resources and we began to
purchase thousands of acres within the continental United
States, and some land outside it to begin producing our own
food. From there we transported this food to our own
supermarkets which we had set up. We experimented with
canning factories, and we are now taking the produce from
our farms into our own canning factories, producing our
own can goods for our own supermarkets. We have gone
into international trade on a small scale, or maybe a large
scale, it depends on how you look at it. We are now the
largest importers of frozen fish in the United States of
America. Last year we imported over twenty-two million
pounds of fish into this country, which we distributed in
the ghettoes to our people. We have entered into trade with
the government of Morocco in North Africa and we have
begun the importation of 500,000 tins of sardines each

month. This is going to increase as we increase our trade with our brothers and sisters around the world. It is the success of our economics that has enabled us to support our school system. We have forty-six universities of Islam in America that we are supporting. Again, the success of the Nation of Islam can be measured by the fact that we have almost wiped out drug taking, divorce, family break-up, vandalism and indiscipline in school, which are still rampant in the White society.

Africa: Why is it that your members do not participate in the political system, and will that attitude change?

Farrakhan: I cannot speak for tomorrow, but as for now, we don't believe that the corrupt political system of White America can solve the problems of Black people. We believe that the way we're going about it will bring about a solution.

Africa: Since the death of the Honourable Elijah Muhammad, there have been several important changes in the Nation of Islam. Whites are no longer singled out as the enemies of Black people, women have been given more responsibilities and the Nation has announced a worldwide mission. Why have you made those changes?

Farrakhan: They are not sudden. We are not today what we were yesterday, nor shall we be tomorrow what we are today. This is the success of the Nation of Islam. Nobody has been able to write about us without his writings becoming stale within a few years. We are an evolving nation that is in accord with the natural laws of growth and development. Honourable Wallace D. Muhammad is giving us a profound teaching on women in general. He has said to us that all over the world women have suffered because of misinterpretations of the scriptures. Society has always worked against the true freedom of women, and that is chiefly because society has been ordered by men. But, women have brilliant minds, and if their minds can be developed and nourished with the right food, they will make an important contribution to the development of society.

So, the Black woman must be liberated from the false ideas that have been instilled in her. Coming to your other point, the Honourable Master Elijah Muhammad taught us that White people were devils. However, what the Honourable Wallace D. Muhammad is doing is refining the language. The problem is not the White people as such, not the people you see in the flesh, but a mentality of lies, tricks, and of falsehood which is used to divide, rule, conquer, subdue and crush the legitimate aspirations of human beings. That is the devil, and it can be any flesh, Black, White, Brown or Yellow. It is that refinement of the teaching of the Honourable Master Elijah Muhammad that you are seeing in the Nation of Islam today.

Africa: Could you be more specific. Why has the Nation of Islam decided to open its membership to White people?

Farrakhan: Because we are Muslims. What Black America failed to take into consideration was our legitimate claim on Islam as our religion. We taught Blackness because we had been victimized by Whiteness, and the germ of Blackness had to be given to the sick mentality of Black people who had been given a White racist philosophy supported by Christianity. In order to bring the Black man out of that, we offered him another extreme, but that extreme is not good either. It was necessary to correct the White mentality. Now, we have to bring the Black racist mentality to a balanced mentality where it will not be hung up on the external composition of the human family, but will rather look at the mind that dwells within that composition. We do not in a true brotherhood recognise colour class nor national origin. We who had all those hang-ups had to be given an antidote. What we were given as an antidote was poison but, it was necessary to restore some harmonious balance to the mind so that we could put on that mind the true divine message of Islam.

Africa: What has been the community's response to the admission of White people to the Temple?

Farrakhan: All the natural things that we would expect

from a people still revolving in the womb of emotions. But you see, the Nation of Islam is not a political movement that keeps its head to the ground listening to the pulsating rhythm of mass thinking. We listen to the dictates of Allah as found in his scriptures and we move according to the time. The Nation of Islam has always been in the vanguard of the thinking of the Black community. When the Black community arrives at one stage of development where they think they have got the Nation of Islam down, we move on to another level that shakes up the Black community. We are always a step ahead, not behind. . . .

Africa: Could you tell us how strong the Nation is in terms of membership?

Farrakhan: He [supreme minister] didn't give the figures in Chicago, but he did say that since January of . . . [1975] three quarters of a million people have come in and out of the Temples of Islam, and since he has been in office 39,000 new converts have registered.

Africa: Could you elaborate on the nature of the Nation's world mission? What do you hope to achieve?

Farrakhan: We believe that the divine mission of the prophets of Almighty God has not been completed on earth. However, three great religious communities have evolved from the teachings of the prophets; namely the Jews, the Christians, and the Muslims. We believe that the religious mission of all great prophets and those great communities has faltered. It didn't falter from the prophets' end; it faltered in the communities carrying out the prophecies. We believe that we, the Black people in America, who have been conditioned by time and human suffering, and who have known the depths of human poverty like no other people have ever known, have been divinely prepared to complete the mission of all the prophets. That mission is to erase all divisions among men by showing the world that all the prophets and their messages are one, and that humanity is one.

Africa: How do you intend to carry out this mission?

Farrakhan: The same way that the Nation is moving now. This is not a thing that you accomplish in the span of a lifetime. The Honourable Master Elijah Muhammad, (may peace be upon him) worked 43 long hard years among us. Yet there are Black people in every city in America who don't even know that the man lived. Now his son has picked up the mantle, our children will pick it up after us. . . .

Africa: How do you answer critics who point out that, historically speaking, Muslims have been among the most vigorous slave traders on the African continent, yet we are told that through Islam the Black man can find freedom in the United States of America?

Farrakhan: The Black man is finding freedom in America through Islam, and the Black man will find freedom in Africa through Islam. When Islam was introduced into Africa during the time shortly after the life of the Prophet Mohammed, it was not an enslaving religion. It was a force that Black Africa used to build some of its great civilizations. In America today it is not Christianity that is inspiring Black people to strive for freedom. We can't condone slavery no matter who is involved in it, but it is only a fool who would negate the wise usage of the atom simply because some beasts dropped it on human beings.

TRANSCENDENTAL MEDITATION [5]

After passing through an era dominated by rationalism, Western culture is experiencing an explosion of religious mysticism—a manifestation of the human spirit's seeking to transcend the confines of the single-storied universe into

[5] From "The Secular Selling of a Religion," by George E. La More Jr., head, department of religion and philosophy, and chairman, division of humanities, Iowa Wesleyan College. *Christian Century.* 92:1133–7. D. 10, '75. Copyright 1975 by Christian Century Foundation. Reprinted by permission from the December 10, 1975 issue of *The Christian Century.*

which it has locked itself since the Enlightenment. Early seasons of mysticism are given to excesses of thrill-seeking and the occult. Satan cults, witchcraft, astrology, charismatic movements—these are often shallow expressions of what may be nonetheless a healthy hunger in the human spirit: the hunger to outgrow the cramped quarters of a shrunken perspective.

One of the most successful responses to this spiritual hunger is Transcendental Meditation (TM). [The late German psychiatrist and philosopher] Karl Jaspers . . . labeled as escapism a great deal of the current interest in Oriental religion and philosophy, especially on the part of young people. The grass always looks greener in distant cultures when youth is fed up with its own. Hence Transcendental Meditation not only speaks to timely hungers but also carries an attractive forwarding address—east of Suez. TM's chief guru, the Maharishi Mahesh Yogi, claims that the discipline of life renewal that he teaches is not really a religion at all but a psychological self-help program which pays all the dividends of religion without the embarrassing urgency and theology. In this way both religious hungers and secular biases are served.

The Guru's Avenue to a Fuller Life

The Maharishi achieved prominence in the West in 1967 when such notables as the Beatles, Mia Farrow and the Beach Boys traveled to India to "find themselves" with the help of the guru. It was not long before many of their followers became his followers. The Maharishi holds a degree in physics from the University of Allahabad, but as a young man he abandoned scientific study of the material world to begin his pilgrimage toward spiritual understanding. (This point may help to explain why he uses the word "scientific" to describe his enlightenment.) His studies with the Guru Dev were followed by a two-year period of meditation in a Himalayan cave—standard fieldwork for guru studies—and after that, a season of travels alone in the forests of India. In the mid-1950s the Maharishi decided to take the insights he had gained out into the world.

With elaborate claims that he and his teacher, the Guru Dev, had discovered a new avenue to a fuller life, the Maharishi Mahesh Yogi came to America for the first time in 1959. He dictated his first book, *Science of Being and the Art of Living (SBAL)*, on a tape recorder at Lake Arrowhead in southern California. Since that visit, more than a quarter of a million Americans have been initiated into TM; an estimated 15,000 per month are brought into the fellowship through 200 recruitment centers strategically located across the country. Set fees are charged upon entrance: $125.00 for an adult; $45.00 for a student. A nonprofit, tax-exempt institution for education with its legal charter in California, the TM organization grosses $6 million a year in income from fees alone. Add to that the sale of publications and fees for advanced studies, and the total is even more impressive.

TM's essential device is the act of meditation (in a relaxed position, eyes closed, two 20-minute periods a day) upon a *mantra*—a Sanskrit word specially chosen for the individual believer which he recites over and over. The Sanskrit mantras when translated may be as disappointing as Italian opera in translation—words like *wheel, bedpost, bridge* and *collar* abound—but in Sanskrit the mantra is claimed by one's trainer to have the right nuance of sound and meaning for the believer. The euphonic repetition is said to cleanse more than focus the mind, thus permitting new intelligence to arise. Once one is assigned his own special mantra, he keeps it a closely guarded secret. Such inside secrets and mysteries have long provided cohesion in Eastern spiritual communities.

The practice of Transcendental Meditation is said to lead first to "transcendental-consciousness"; this in turn opens out into "cosmic-consciousness." Ultimately—and this is quite a bonus for a group claiming to be nonreligious—one arrives at "God-consciousness." The final state is not fully accomplished in this lifetime: reincarnation is an integral part of the Maharishi's beliefs.

Scientific Studies of TM

The Student International Meditation Society (SIMS), active on more than 1,000 campuses, emphasizes the secular, nonreligious identity of the movement, calling it a "science" and compiling dramatic studies of improvements in metabolism, blood pressure, cerebral alpha and theta wave production under the influence of Transcendental Meditation. It is SIMS which has founded the Maharishi International University, located initially in Santa Barbara, California, and now in Fairfield, Iowa. . . .

The list of benefits attributed to regular Transcendental Meditation—20 minutes with one's mantra, twice a day—is reminiscent of the labels on bottles of "snake oil" sold from medicine wagons in former days: improvements in metabolism and blood pressure, relaxation from anxiety, clearer and more creative consciousness, improved social relations. Adherents of TM claim benefits ranging from the shrinkage of ulcers to an improved sex life.

Elaborate scientific studies have measured both physiological and psychological changes in persons during the practice of TM. This large body of literature has been called into question by researchers with names as notable as those who did the original studies. Keith Wallace, appointed president of MIU in Santa Barbara, was a pioneer in such research with his doctor's thesis in the physiology of TM, published in *Science* in 1970. He carefully documented his finding that persons in a state of TM reduce their oxygen consumption by 20 per cent, and both their skin sensitivity and mental responsiveness increase with this metabolic slowdown. The most controversial claim is that TM causes an "increase of creative intelligence."

The Maharishi sometimes claims that the Guru Dev and he have discovered a new path to human betterment—and at other times indicates that they have actually updated something very ancient. His emphasis seems to be on the former claim; the evidence rests with the latter. The act of meditation upon mantras is one of the oldest devices in the Vedic tradition of Hinduism. It is not altogether different from the Sufi mysticism of Islam known as *Zikr*, in which mantras are crucial.

Over the centuries much has been learned about such meditation. Typical human consciousness is diffuse—scattered over many simultaneous concerns. We seldom give our fullest attention to anything. Now, the practice of concentration on a single idea—be it a mantra, a Hail Mary or a portion of the Lord's Prayer—does cultivate the capacity truly to give one's total mind to one thing at one time. And once this capacity is developed, it can be transferred to other matters. A person who develops the capacity of focused attention finds a greater sense of equilibrium and power in the management of his affairs.

Similarly, it has long been known that meditation on a single object, idea or sound not only causes other stimuli to recede to the vanishing point; after a time the focused object of meditation also seems to be called away, leaving a focused point of nothingness or "pure consciousness," as it is known in such traditions as Zen Buddhism. Psychologists such as Robert Ornstein have long been fascinated by this phenomenon. It is into this emptiness of the head that pure, creative intelligence arises, according to the Maharishi Mahesh Yogi.

The Selling of TM

As unlikely as all of this speculation may sound to busy Americans, TM has been admirably packaged and commercialized with them in mind. Americans have long shown an affinity for transcendental musings in the tradition of Thoreau, Emerson, Bronson Alcott and Whitman. . . .

Ideally American is the idea of a single payment ($125.00/$45.00) with no regular dues ("Nobody will call"). Similarly, the "soft" conversion expected of believers hardly calls for a person to change his habits at all, but for the two painless 20-minute periods a day, out of which come new life.

Furthermore, in a season of enormous complexity the sheer programmed simplicity of TM has its appeal. Here is a faith with the precise steps of a computer program. . . .

And yet TM is a very definite religion in a very definite disguise. Whatever the scientific benefits of TM, its religious functions become clear in the Maharishi's claim that "Transcendental Meditation is a path to God." . . . "A very good form of prayer is this meditation which leads us in the field of the Creator, to the source of Creation, to the field of God." . . . Even minus its God-talk, TM offers a total philosophy of life renewal and a plan of salvation for the world ("world plan"). Religion by any other name is still religion. . . .

The Maharishi and his followers claim that even at its highest theological level, TM is totally compatible with all religions, and hence is not itself *a religion*. It is highly questionable, however, whether the faith described in TM could ever square with the Christian vision of a personal God, or the primacy of Christ and the eternal, indissoluble worth of persons as they achieve their personhood in a single lifetime on earth. Instead, there is presented the diffuse monism of Brahma, a religion of mystical thought rather than historical encounter. And the reincarnation of persons is affirmed in the personal faith of the Maharishi to the degree that one's current, distinctive individuality has no permanent worth. Such a faith is hardly compatible with the basic religions of the West—Judaism, Christianity and Islam.

ATHEISTS: SOCIETY OF SEPARATIONISTS [6]

A few score atheists held a convention in New York City and found that it is not easy for serious atheists to attract attention at a time when there is so little serious religion around, rather like trying to play handball without a wall.

[6] From " 'There Are No Churches for Atheists,' " by Walter Goodman, staff editor. New York *Times Magazine*. p 16–17. My. 16, '76. © 1976 by The New York Times Company. Reprinted by permission.

They composed a middle-class, middle-aged extraordinarily ordinary group and comported themselves more decorously than stockholders at many a corporation's annual meeting. . . .

Two recent graduates from the University of Delaware, who had come hoping for an opportunity to discuss the nicer points of religion with their peers, found themselves substantively as well as generationally out of things and spent more time in the vestibule than in the ballroom where the speeches were being made. One of them recalled that he had been converted to atheism at a Moravian camp when he was 13. "The minister persuaded me. He told me that you can only get to heaven by grace, not by good works. I couldn't accept it on account of my grandmother. My grandmother was really a nice person. If she could be sent to hell, I decided I'd rather go to hell with her."

But the meeting did not touch on such matters. The emphasis was political, practical and social, not theological. A young mother was there to declare herself against laws prohibiting abortion. A librarian from Illinois was upset by the difficulty of getting books about atheism into her library. A Michigan man was troubled by the judge in Detroit who permitted a statue of the Virgin Mary to be set up in his courtroom. A New Jersey man was indignant that signs such as "Turn left for the Episcopal Church" are permitted on the portion of the curb that belongs to the town, and he has complained to his local post office about "Pray for Peace" cancellations. A Massachusetts man was there frankly for comradeship—"to be with my fellow atheists." Several of the congregants remarked on how rarely they got the opportunity to share their beliefs. "There are very few people I can talk to at home," sighed the librarian. Another woman observed, not entirely as a joke, "There are no churches for atheists."

The meeting passed quietly; the atheists staged no protest marches, picketed no churches. In an era when militancy is the hallmark of any self-respecting minority, America's atheists have not managed to invade the nation's consciousness. For all one knows, they may be more than a minority; a lot of people would be hard put to tell . . . [a pollster], or themselves, whether they believe in God. It has always taken a certain audacity to say or think flatly, where He might overhear, "I don't believe," and even unbelievers who are able to utter those words in a congregation of the similarly minded, such as the weekend meeting at the New York Sheraton Hotel, are likely to be constrained back home by the reception they can anticipate from neighbors, employers, fellow workers, customers, clients and passers-by.

The conspicuous exception to this image of the prudent atheist, of course, is Mrs. Madalyn Murray O'Hair, founder and president for life of the Society of Separationists (S.O.S.), which sponsored last month's meeting, the body's sixth annual convention and its first in New York. The aggressive, articulate, energetic, enterprising, informed and forthcoming Mrs. O'Hair first won national vilification and victory in 1963 with her suit to eliminate prayer from the public schools. Since then, she has been engaged in what she calls a campaign of "litigious education," designed to draw the citizenry's attention to the special privileges granted religious bodies despite the provision of the First Amendment to the Constitution that "Congress shall make no law respecting an establishment of religion, or prohibiting the free exercise thereof." Mrs. O'Hair and her organization are dedicated to "the complete and absolute separation of church and state."

What this slogan means can be gathered from a sampling of her many targets: the exemption from taxation enjoyed by religious bodies; the tax funds which find their way to parochial schools; prayer breakfasts at the White House; all statutes regulating divorce, abortion, homosexual encounters and any other variety of behavior on the grounds that it offends some religious sect or precept; crosses as part of Christmas decorations in Federal buildings; the officially programmed spontaneous moment of prayer by the Apollo 8 astronauts as they circled the earth. (She didn't mind the astronauts' praying, but she claims they were ordered to pray by NASA and she objected to their doing it out loud over a world hookup and on company time.) At present, she is trying to raise $200,000 to hire a top-quality law firm, instead of the "turkey lawyers" she has generally had to settle for, to fight two cases—one to bar the Department of Health, Education and Welfare from allocating educational funds to states that have moved to bring prayer back into the public schools; the other to prevent the U.S. Treasury from granting aid to states that have a religious test for employment, even unto a "So help me God" at swearing-in ceremonies.

She is not unrealistic about her chances: "The U.S. Supreme Court is shot to hell. This is a symbolic war—that we sure as hell are losing." In the decade since her battle against school prayer, Mrs. O'Hair, now 57, has grown larger and grayer, but the face beneath the bangs is youthful, as alive as it was in the days when defenders of religion in Baltimore were breaking her windows and slashing her tires and posting obscenity-garnished letters wishing her and her family painful deaths. She talks at a peppy pace, the sentences well marshaled, the sincerity indubitable, the sentiments unequivocal: "You cannot close down the schools for Easter and Christmas and Passover and Hanukkah unless you also close them for the great natural atheist holidays, two at the equinox, two at the solstice season. . . . People in trouble are being handed over by the Federal Government to religious institutions. The Office of Economic Opportunity ought to be called the Office of Ecclesiastical Opportunity. Unfortunately, most of the homes for wayward girls are in the hands of the Catholic Church. They ought to be secular, but nobody has the brains to see it. . . . If you go into a hospital for an appendectomy, you have to tell them what religion you are before they'll take out the appendix. If you say you're an atheist, they'll send for a minister to look at the appendix first. . . . We'll attack any candidate who oversteps the line between church and state. We gave George Wallace good marks for wanting to tax churches, bad marks for holding prayer services in the state Capitol. Carter thinks he has a personal relationship with God, but there's no candidate out there for the atheists."

The Society of Separationists, based in Austin, Tex., is a combination of Mrs. O'Hair, a handful of relatives and friends, and a claimed mailing list of 70,000 mostly inactive families. According to Mrs. O'Hair, it has attracted a disproportionate number of Republicans and Jews, as well as small-business men, engineers and veterinarians. "Every goddam vet in the country must be an atheist." She believes that at least a quarter of the nation is made up of practicing atheists, and she has set herself the job of "getting closet atheists out of the closet."

She dismisses the conversion of the religious as waste effort: "Religious people are throwaway people." And she has scant sympathy for persons who whisper their support for her crusades yet make a public show of piety. When a doctor who tithed religiously to his church came to her back door in Maryland one night to offer $200 in cash for her school-prayer fight, she told him what unprintable thing he could do with his money. Nor do most kinds of atheists fall into her good graces. She categorizes them by species:

☐ Primitive atheists—"People who come of age, look at Christianity and find it incredible, as any sensible person would, and eventually join the Unitarians or Ethical Culturists. They don't like to get mixed up in physical combat."

☐ Hate atheists—"They cite the number of incidents of priests living with housekeepers, or ministers making indecent advances on choir boys. They may move on to astrology."

☐ Philosophical atheists—"They get bogged down in reading holy books, the Torah, the King James Bible, the [Hindu] Upanishads, [Christian Science] *Science and Health*. These people use up precious time analyzing trash and writing genteel, erudite and worthless articles, and join the American Humanist Association."

☐ Fanatical atheists—"They all convert from Jehovah's Witnesses."

☐ Sectarian atheists—"They love internecine strife. There are now 12 or 13 atheist organizations in the country which do nothing but fight each other."

Mrs. O'Hair's favorite kind of atheist, presumably represented by the few score people at the Sheraton, are "grounded in life, with a freewheeling, open-ended philosophy that emphasizes the worth of the individual. They trust reason, experience and common sense, not creeds, rituals or dogmas. They bend no knee and bow no head. They are as negative as Columbus, who believed the world was not flat. They are as destructive as Galileo, who destroyed misconceptions about the universe. They are as anti as a physician who cures a disease." . . . Most people [at the convention] seemed very pleased to be there, to see Madalyn O'Hair in person, . . . to hear atheism extolled in the ballroom of a big hotel, perhaps to wear for a few days the atheist medallion (an A superimposed on a pattern of electrons), which they will not have much occasion to wear in the offices, shops, bars and bowling alleys back home. "In a small town," said an Indiana man, "you can't afford to be an atheist."

For a number of these atheists, perhaps most of them, the end of the convention meant a return to the closet. Mrs. Secular dashed away in panic when she noticed that I was jotting down her name. A former minister had difficulty in bringing himself to explain what he was doing at the Sheraton: "I'm still a Presbyterian. I am not an atheist. I am interested in criticism from atheists or anybody else. I participate in criticism. I'm sympathetic to atheists. My philosophy is existential. God! Let the chips fall where they may—I am an atheist." He gathered up the chips and asked that his name not be published since he is still collecting a pension from the Presbyterians.

The man who was given a charter at the meeting to organize a New York chapter, a former theology student whose conversion began when he saw *Inherit the Wind* [a

play and film that deal with a Scopes trial-like situation]
preferred that his name not be published because he makes
his living playing an organ in a church. The organizer of the
New Jersey chapter, sporting a tax-the-churches button,
didn't mind being known as an atheist as long as the fact
was not connected with the gas station he runs. The elderly
organizer of the Florida chapter had not felt able to declare
himself an atheist until a few years ago when he retired, as
a captain, from the New York City police force: "All I had
to do was announce myself as an atheist and I'd've
stopped being a cop." There are only a half dozen operating
S.O.S. chapters, and most of them are barely operating. The
problem, according to Mrs. O'Hair, is economic pressure:
"Only a self-sufficient businessman or a retired person dares
take on the public role of organizer."

We may draw at least two conclusions from the recent
convention: (1) Tomorrow's stock of positive atheists is
related directly to today's stock of seminarians. (2) Potential
proselytizers for atheism have learned that persons who
avow a lack of faith are treated in most cities and towns as
members of an eccentric if not dangerous class, no matter
that they are demonstrably less dangerous and much less
eccentric than the disciples of numerous religious cults.
Mrs. O'Hair was turned into a media freak—the "strident"
Madalyn O'Hair—for saying more reasonable things than
Billy Graham, although in lustier language, being no more
fanatic about her beliefs than the preachers in the churches
where Jimmy Carter prays, and showing much more courage
than most of the people who by and large agree with her
on the issues. "The ground moves under liberals' feet,"
she says with some bitterness. "They disappear into the
woodwork."

Even among those at the meeting who were unqualifiedly
willing to go on record for their beliefs and man the barri-
cades if need be, there was a sense that their cause might do
better if they personally remained apart from the fight. The
1975 Atheist of the Year, an Indiana phone-company owner
who had a cross burned on his lawn after he instituted a

Dial-an-Atheist service where callers could hear jokes about "Sky Daddy" and "Holy Spook," has learned to keep out of civil-liberties controversies lest his presence scare off potential supporters.

The gathering of atheists at the Sheraton was humorous in the way that gatherings of the unconventional generally are, but I found something disquieting in the realization that people who historically have done little harm compared with zealots operating under supernatural auspices, who can lay fair claim to having science and the U.S. Constitution on their side, who are entirely law-abiding—that these people in a society we are pleased to think of as secular should nonetheless have such good reason to feel themselves to be pariahs.

The Sixth National Annual Convention of American Atheists, which began without a benediction, ended without a prayer.

WOMEN ORDAINED [7]

Bishop Donald J. Davis turned to the congregation of All Saints Episcopal Church in Indianapolis last week and asked: "Is it your will that Jacqueline be ordained a priest?" The answer was a rousing "It is"—and with the laying on of hands, Jacqueline Means, a 40-year-old nurse and prison chaplain, became the first woman officially admitted to the priesthood of the U.S. Episcopal Church. But the historic ceremony was marked by protest. As the service was getting under way, Robert Strippy, representing the conservative American Church Union, rose to denounce Means's ordination as "an act of heresy opposed to the mind of the church and the will of God." With that, a small band of sympathizers marched out in protest.

Though the General Convention of the Episcopal Church voted to admit women to the priesthood . . . [in 1976] the effective date was delayed until . . . [January

[7] From article by Margaret Montagno and Laurie Lisle, staff writers. *Newsweek*. 89:85. Ja. 17, '77. Copyright 1977 by Newsweek, Inc. All rights reserved. Reprinted by permission.

1977]. Last week, more than a dozen women were ordained, including the first black woman, 66-year-old constitutional lawyer Pauli Murray. And with about 30 more women to be ordained this month, the issue that brought the first serious threat of schism in U.S. Anglican history is now being tested. The Coalition for the Apostolic Ministry (CAM), a group that includes twelve bishops, met in Chicago last month to work for repeal of the new laws. The traditionalist Fellowship of Concerned Churchmen (FCC) is threatening schism. And one church, St. Mary's in Denver, has already seceded and labeled itself an "independent Anglican parish."

Discord

The women ordained deplore the conflict, but remain firm in their cause. "It bothers me that the church is in discord now," says Means. "But nobody ever said it was easy to be a Christian." Several of the women, like the Rev. Alice Mann of Philadelphia, are married to priests, but only a few, like Carol Anderson of New York, have parish posts. And while the women have been warmly received, the controversy continues. This week, Bishop Paul Moore of New York will ordain Ellen Marie Barrett, 30, an avowed lesbian.

The 3,000-member CAM is pledged to work for reform within the church. CAM's director, the Rev. James Wattley, has sent letters of protest to every bishop in the country, but with typical Anglican sense of propriety, the group shuns unseemly demonstrations. "When women celebrate the Holy Eucharist or give a blessing, we will try not to be present to avoid an embarrassing situation when we have to walk out," says Wattley. Hard-liners like the FCC also argue for boycotting services held by women. But the FCC is calling for an out-and-out break and will hold a meeting next fall to consider forming a separate church body.

The rebels at Denver's St. Mary's, who voted to secede last November, continue to hold services in their church.

Their pastor, forbidden by his bishop to function as a priest, says he has contacted 40 to 50 other sympathetic clergymen for support. But the secession has saddened the community and split some families within the parish. Richard Atchison voted not to secede, while his wife voted to leave. "The decision has been rough on us," says Theda Atchison, "but I feel I've grown spiritually. After all, I have nothing to lose and heaven to gain."

Male Bastions

Since no bishop has to ordain a woman against his will and no church will be forced to accept a woman priest, the hierarchy hopes to avoid major conflict. Presiding bishop John Maury Allin, who admits he is not "convinced theologically" of the validity of women priests, says he will simply encourage dissenters to seek out all-male bastions. Even some conservatives seem resigned to losing the battle. "I would not leave the Church unless they threw me out," says Stuart Casper, a member of the American Church Union.

That attitude—and the kind of compromise now being worked out in the Chicago diocese—could preserve Episcopal unity. Bishop James Montgomery is opposed to women priests; his assistant bishop Quintin Primo Jr. is not. When it comes time for Chicago Anglicans to ordain a woman, Bishop Montgomery let it be known recently that he will see to it that Bishop Primo does the ordaining.

RELIGION AND THE EQUAL RIGHTS AMENDMENT [8]

The attitudes of American churches toward the Equal Rights Amendment (ERA) are at once puzzling and ironic. Take the Christian churches: given their religion's professed concern for human rights, ERA should, on the face of it, be a natural cause for these churches to support.

[8] From "Confusion Among the Faithful," by Martin E. Marty, professor of the history of modern Christianity, University of Chicago. *Saturday Review.* 4:10–11. Je. 25, '77. Reprinted by permission.

Yet matters haven't worked out that way. The major Christian groups either differ sharply on the amendment or ignore it altogether. Surprisingly, there seems to be no single doctrinal touchstone capable of resolving these differences in approach. In fact, the divergences between the churches that *have* taken a "pro" or "anti" position seem to turn less on theology than on such secular considerations as regional traditions and political ideology.

The Sunbelt—which is also the Churchbelt—stretching from the Deep South to Arizona, is the anti-ERA stronghold. The huge Southern Baptist Convention dominates there. True, a million or more Baptists may be linked with that denomination's best-known family, the Jimmy Carters, in support of ratification; but no one speaks for the entire body of the fiercely congregational Southern Baptists. Their Christian Life Commission (CLC) often speaks *to* them, but CLC spokesman Foy Valentine reports that organized Southern Baptist groups have not spoken up for the ERA or even taken it up. Understandably, he would also like it known that the noisiest opposition to ERA comes from the rightist fringe of the convention or from fundamentalists beyond the Southern Baptist borders. Old southern ideas about womanhood or ladyhood and old-fashioned constitutional conservatism may be chiefly responsible for anti-ERA sentiment on Baptist turf.

On the Sunbelt's border lie Utah and Colorado, the former a Latter-Day Saint, or Mormon, precinct, the latter a Mormon spillover territory that vigorously opposed the amendment a few months ago. Did not God predestine male-female differences to last through eternity? What would the ERA do to the father's power and to family life (Mormons are big on families), or to sex differentiation in the churches?

In the opposite camp are the United Methodists, who are also strong in states reluctant to ratify. Their national General Conference has supported the ERA since 1972, and most regional and local boards and bureaus have spoken up for it. The leadership of the 1.2-million-member

women's division of Methodism recently asked their fellow
Methodists, by a 70—3 vote, to avoid vacationing in these
slow-to-ratify states.

In the ratifying states, Catholics, Jews, and "mainline
Protestants" are strong. Catholics, who used to make up
what comedian Lenny Bruce called "the only *The* Church,"
today are less a voting bloc than a two-party system. Pro-
ERA Catholics find plenty of support in Vatican II and
recent papal documents favoring equal rights and justice,
but the Church has taken no stand. The Colorado battles
found the Catholic Right busy against the ERA, with the
Knights of Columbus and "Pro-Life" forces trying to link
ERA with legalized abortion. Perhaps the most vocal anti-
amendment speaker is the tireless Phyllis Schlafly, who
finds Catholic arguments for her stand.

An organization called the Religious Committee for the
Equal Rights Amendment has attracted 19 signatory groups,
drawn from liberals and mainliners. To the left within the
coalition are Unitarian Universalists, Friends, and the like.
Vastly outnumbering them are the more moderate Church
Women United, Lutheran Church Women, Church of the
Brethren (and Sistren?), American Baptists, United Church
of Christ, National Council of Churches, and sundry Presbyterian—including largely southern Presbyterian—representatives. The United Presbyterian Church in the U.S.A. supported the ERA in its General Assembly in 1970, 1974, and
1975. But the mainline churches lack some of their old
power and zest at the moment. They lost some Sunday
soldiers after the Sixties; the survivors are a bit gun-shy
about social issues and seem tired of being seen as generals
without armies, leadership without followership. A tinge of
wariness and apathy accompanies their support.

Three groups that divide over the idea of ordaining
women to the ministry have different attitudes toward the
ERA. Jews are redrawing traditional sex-differentiating
lines in the synagogue while their support of equal rights
in the world around them seems unflagging. The Missouri Lutherans, the last major Lutheran holdouts on the

"Women's Ordination" front, will this summer receive a "Theological Document" that calls members to seek justice and rights, but leans against ERA on grounds that sound like those of the Mormons. Probably most Episcopalians have favored ratification, but they have been too busy with internal affairs to take it up as a group. Even a "Women's Triennial" of the Episcopal folk did not have the amendment on the agenda.

However much leaders may bustle about on both sides of this issue, readers of the denominational press or observers of congregational life are likely to walk away with one clear impression: Equal rights for women commands a lower priority than equal rights for racial minorities did. Cautious or numbed, most church people seem to cherish the sidelines, while Methodist women advocate selective tourism and the Mormons and Phyllis Schlafly line up against the amendment in the name of their God and His—and they do mean His—sex-differentiating preferences.

V. YOUTH AND RELIGION

EDITOR'S INTRODUCTION

During the late 1960s and early 1970s, there was a succession of notable and newsworthy causes that attracted large numbers of young people in the United States—the civil rights movement, opposition to the war in Vietnam, and concern for the environment, to name the principal ones. Coming to the fore in the middle and late 1970s has been the involvement of the young in the "cause" of religion.

Like older Americans, young people display no uniformity in their religious preferences. Their involvement has primarily taken two forms: one is their attachment to the evangelical movement, discussed in Section II; the other is their conversion to a variety of religions or movements having their origin in the Asian world.

The first selection, by Kenneth and Elizabeth Woodward, seeks to determine what is behind this interest and participation. The next two selections describe some of the cults that attract the young as their principal adherents. Finally, Harvey Cox, the noted theologian, discusses some of the legal aspects of the youth-oriented cults.

TEENAGERS TURN TO RELIGION [1]

For a young woman nineteen years old, Jennifer Webb has made a lot of "trips" in her life. There was the drug trip at sixteen, the sex trip at seventeen and several trips

[1] From "Why Are Teens Turning to Religion?" by Kenneth L. Woodward and Elizabeth Woodward. *Seventeen.* 34:96–7+. Jl. '75. Reprinted from *Seventeen* ® Magazine. Copyright © 1975 by Triangle Communications Inc. All rights reserved. Kenneth L. Woodward is religion editor of *Newsweek*; Elizabeth Woodward, a freelance journalist.

to a family counselor before Jennifer discovered what she calls "the ultimate trip." "It's God," says Jennifer, casually tossing her long blond hair back from her radiant face.

Jennifer is a freshman at a junior college in upstate New York, but if you ask her what she's into, she'll tell you it's religion. For more than a year now, she has been meeting three times a week and twice on weekends with a group of some fifty "born-again Christians," as they call themselves, for Bible study, intense prayer and cheerful spiritual counseling. Jennifer's bearded boy friend, Lenny, is in the group. So are all of her best campus friends. When she finishes her studies in speech therapy, Jennifer plans to devote her entire life to God, her family and her career—in that order.

Jennifer is one of millions of young Americans who have made the search for God in the 1970s what civil rights and the antiwar movement were to millions of equally restless, questioning students in the 1960s. Not all these young people are turning to Christianity or Judaism. Unlike their parents, they have a whole spiritual smorgasbord to choose from—various forms of Buddhism, Islam, Hinduism, as well as a host of minor sects and exotic cults. In fact, where missionaries from the United States once went abroad to convert others to Christianity, this country has itself become missionary territory for hundreds of gurus, self-proclaimed messiahs and other religious zealots anxious to feed many of the young people who have developed a genuine hunger for God.

To put the current religious scene into perspective, it is useful to remember that ten years ago a group of Protestant theologians shocked religious Americans with their dramatic announcement, "God is dead." What they meant was that the very idea of God had become irrelevant, unnecessary and uninspiring. At the same time, public opinion polls showed that increasing numbers of Americans were, in fact, staying away from church and losing confidence in organized religion.

Today, however, opinion polls seem to tell a different

story. [See "Profound Religious Revival," in Section I, above.] . . .

Even so, the youth movements of the sixties have produced enormous changes in the kind of religious services conventional Christian churches now offer the young. The Jesus Movement, which began outside the churches among college and high school students, has found a home in the seventies among Baptist and other conservative Protestant denominations, where ministers in long hair and modish clothes encourage young people to pour out their newfound faith through informal rap sessions and country-western spirituals like *Gospel Road*. A similar youth orientation is evident in the popular folk masses which have become a Sunday feature in many Roman Catholic parishes, and in the use of guitars, dancing and unusual visual art forms in many Episcopal and Lutheran churches. Among transplanted midwesterners in California, Mormon missionaries find whole families anxious to join the Church of Jesus Christ of Latter-Day Saints because of its emphasis on family togetherness. Meanwhile, some young Jews are rediscovering their own traditions in the synagogue and through roving bands of singing, dancing Hassids (members of a mystical orthodox sect) who often visit college campuses.

Going to church, of course, is not the only or even the most useful measure of religious attitudes, especially among the young. "Young people are interested in ritual, but only if it helps them feel closer to God," says Father Andrew Greeley, the noted Catholic sociologist. According to a recent—and highly revealing—survey for the National Opinion Research Center, Father Greeley and his fellow sociologists found that a third of those surveyed have had at least one mystical experience in their lives—a religious experience that has nothing to do with going to church. Moreover, those under twenty were more willing to talk about those experiences than their elders. "Unlike a lot of older people," Greeley reports, "teens have not given up on a God who will make His presence felt in their lives. They think that is what religion is all about."

This search for religious experience, then, appears to

be the main reason why so many teens are interested in religion. It also helps to explain why more than four million Americans, most of them young people, have turned to various forms of Hinduism, Buddhism and other oriental religions which emphasize spiritual techniques for developing a new consciousness of self, the world and God.

Some New Directions

Perhaps the easiest of these techniques to understand is Transcendental Meditation. TM is a simple mental exercise taught by the Maharishi Mahesh Yogi, the bearded Indian guru who has counted among his disciples such well-known figures as the Beatles, football quarterback Joe Namath and cover girl Samantha Jones. [See "Transcendental Meditation," in Section IV, above.] . . .

What often surprises American parents is the willingness—and eagerness—of so many young religion seekers to give up the freedoms and comforts considered essential to the good life, American-style. Nowhere is this self-denial more evident than among the youthful devotees of the International Society for Krishna Consciousness (ISKON), a rigid Buddhist sect founded ten years ago by His Divine Grace A. C. Bhaktivedanta Swami Prabuhpada, a retired Indian businessman. . . .

The sect's essential spiritual exercise is not much different from that of TM: instead of meditating silently, members chant their mantra ("Hare Krishna, Hare Krishna, Krishna Krishna, Hare Hare"), usually to the accompaniment of hand cymbals, clay drums and bare dancing feet. The chant is a form of "worship yoga" dedicated to Lord Krishna, a classic Hindu manifestation of God. The purpose of the chant, and of all the sect's rites and rules, is to develop Krishna's divine consciousness of "absolute reality" among all the sect's members.

What first strikes outsiders about the young followers of Krishna is their unusual costumes. The women wear multicolored saris and the men dress in saffron robes. All males, even infants, have the head shaved except for a single tuft of hair on the back of the skull which, so the legend goes,

Lord Krishna may someday grab to yank them up to heaven.

When they are not out chanting and begging in the streets, devotees of Lord Krishna live frugally in their ashrams, or communes. Most are celibates. Those who do marry are permitted to have sexual intercourse only once a month at precisely the optimum time for conception, and even married couples must cease all sexual activity by the age of thirty. Couples who do produce children must give them up when they reach the age of five. At that point, all Krishna children are sent to the sect's Gurukula, a special boarding school housed in a former Christian church in East Dallas, Texas, where they are raised as wards of the entire community.

Why do some young Americans choose such an ascetic life? "To serve God and dwell in his consciousness," says Belinda, a shy young woman who refused to give her family name or exact age. "Once you realize Krishna Consciousness, you want it for your children too. We teach them to love God and avoid contaminated environments," she says, meaning most of the attractions of the conventional American way of life.

Along with mystical experience, many young people today also want religion to provide them with a total philosophy of life (something they apparently cannot find at home or in school) and an authority figure they can trust to show them what is right and wrong.

"I think this interest in religion has a lot to do with a rejection of parental permissiveness," says George Williamson, a college professor who has seen both his son and daughter leave home to live in separate religious communes. "I must admit that we raised our children without much religion," he acknowledges. "We left it pretty much up to them to decide what, if anything, to believe in. But what we really did, I guess, is train them perfectly for a religious guru who could give them all the answers."

For Williamson's daughter, Margaret, that guru turned out to be the Maharaj-Ji, the seventeen-year-old Perfect Master of the Divine Light Mission. Margaret lives in one of the Mission's fifty-odd ashrams in the United States, where she scrubs floors beneath a sign which reads "God is great, but greater is Guru because he holds the key to God." Like most gurus, the Maharaj-Ji teaches his devotees a special spiritual technique, which he calls The Knowledge. In a secret rite, initiates learn to see a dazzling white light, hear celestial music and feel ecstatic vibrations—a total religious experience called "blissing out."

In appreciation for what The Knowledge has given them, the guru's disciples devote their time and money to winning more followers for the Maharaj-Ji. But while his followers live simply in their ashrams, shunning sex, meat and most of the normal comforts of life, the Perfect Master enjoys chauffeured limousines, three separate estates and two airplanes which he uses to fly his "divine family" from one religious rally to another.

A third reason young people are turning to religion is the close family feeling they get from living in a religious group. Indeed, the newest and most bizarre religion in America is... [The Unification Church], a strange mixture of oriental family piety and Protestantism that stresses a good marriage (including lots of children) as the only road to spiritual happiness. Instead of forming congregations, the sect's members (few of the estimated 500,000 United States members are over thirty) form interlocking family units, each devoted to promulgating the gospel of the sect's leader, Dr. Sun Myung Moon.

Dr. Moon is a mysterious South Korean evangelist who has somehow collected enough money to purchase three luxurious estates in New York, including a palatial mansion on the Hudson River for his own family. Wherever Dr. Moon preaches, he busses in thousands of young people who dutifully stand on street corners drumming up an audience for him. Every few years, Dr. Moon stages a mass wedding ceremony, where as many as 750 young couples come from all over the world to exchange marriage vows. This United Family, Dr. Moon teaches, is the advance guard for a new messiah who is to come soon to save the world. And in his lectures, the oriental evangelist makes it rather clear that this world savior could turn out to be Dr. Moon himself.

How can young people distinguish between genuine holy men and cunning rip-offs? Obviously, it isn't easy. But two warnings are worth keeping in mind: true spiritual growth takes a lifetime to achieve; perfect fulfillment is an illusion. What's more, traditional holy men have never lived handsomely off the devotion and offerings of their disciples but have set an example of disdain for creature comforts.

Despite competition from Eastern sects, the religion of most young Americans is still some form of Christianity. The search for mystical experience, a total philosophy of life and a family-style sense of community is also evident among today's young Christians. This is particularly true within the Charismatic, or Pentecostal, movement which is spreading rapidly among both Protestants and Roman Catholics. . . . [See "Charismatic Christians," by K. A. Briggs, in Section II, above.]

A Brighter Hope

Just how far the spiritual revolution of the seventies will spread or how long it will last are questions no one can answer. If past history is any guide, the religious enthusiasm so many young people now display will eventually give way to spiritual flabbiness and another period of secular-life-as-usual. A brighter hope is that their fresh sense of God's presence will invigorate conventional church life and give a new sense of community to those who have grown cool in their faith.

CULTS – MAGNETS FOR YOUTH [2]
Reprinted from *U.S. News & World Report.*

Again many of America's young people are on the move toward a radically different life—not to drugs or rioting as in the 1960s but to religious cults.

[2] From "Religious Cults: Newest Magnet for Youth." *U.S. News & World Report.* 80:52–4. Je. 14, '76.

By the hundreds of thousands, these youths are living and working on behalf of new-found beliefs and leaders.

Such converts can be seen roaming the streets of U.S. cities—selling incense as Oriental monks or singing Gospel hymns and taking up collections.

Many are living in suburban or small-town communes, others in communities of their own in the countryside.

Battle for Loyalty

Their shift often brings a total break from past friends, jobs or studies, and family.

In that situation, a continuing state of hostilities has developed between some of the cults and some parents who believe that their children are being bilked and brainwashed in virtual captivity.

There has been a rash of forcible removals of young people—with or without court orders—from the communes. Officials are looking into some of the cults for tax and other violations.

This growing warfare between conventional America and the cults moved into a new dimension on June 1 at New York City's Yankee Stadium, where 30,000 persons came to see and hear Korean evangelist Sun Myung Moon, head of the Unification Church and a leading figure among the new cultists.

Hecklers tore down decorations and fought with Mr. Moon's followers. The millionaire preacher delivered his speech behind a shield of bulletproof glass to the accompaniment of boos, catcalls and smoke bombs.

At present, anywhere from 1 million to 3 million Americans, mostly in their twenties or late teens, are involved in 200 to 1,000 of these new cults.

Cultism, however, is not a new development in this country.

Over the centuries, narrowly based sects have built up —then usually lost—followings for dogmas and panaceas ranging from free love to snake handling. Hindu mystics at one time or another have done well in the United States.

Few if any such movements, though, centered as strongly on youth as the current ones do.

Today, the nation's "new believers" vary widely—from Oriental meditators to bands of youths waiting in the desert for saviors due to arrive in spaceships from "the same kingdom that Christ came from."

What enables such groups to prosper?

Many religious and social analysts point to a large reservoir of troubled youths in the U.S.—some involved in drugs, and others with traditionally devout views that crack, often in the transition from home to college. These and other youngsters are attracted to the authoritarian image presented by many cult leaders.

For such young people, religious fervor usually runs at a high pitch.

"Warmth" and "Love" Cited

Cultists speak enthusiastically of the "warmth" and "love" they find among fellow members. Mr. Moon's followers, for example, call him "our spiritual father" and call their group "a unified family."

In most religious communities, visitors find a strict routine of lectures and ecstatic prayers. Many cults ban drinking, drugs, nonmarital sex. . . .

Defectors, however, have testified that female members of the Children of God sect were sometimes sexually abused by cult leaders.

It is also charged that millions of dollars raised by the rank and file through begging or work go into the pockets of many cult leaders.

As leaders of parents' protest organizations see it, the young people are enticed into cults' week-end retreats by smiling and affectionate members; then their resistance is weakened by long hours of work, indoctrination and, often, malnutrition. The process, these parents' leaders say, amounts to "psychological kidnaping."

Such charges have not been upheld in court, and cult leaders strongly deny exploiting young members. Mr.

Moon, for instance, says that he keeps for his personal use only part of the sprawling New York estates that his church has bought for training centers as well as a proposed university.

Similarly, the Divine Light Mission asserts that its youthful guru, Maharaj-Ji, pays for his personal possessions —including a string of luxury cars—from voluntary gifts outside church channels.

A number of experts have voiced skepticism about critics' charges that brainwashing is employed by the cults. Herbert Hendin, a Columbia University psychoanalyst who studies youth movements for the Center for Policy Research, reports:

"I've never seen one of these young people who didn't have some kind of serious failure in family life.

"They're turning desperately from the pain of the outside world to the childlike support and structures of a make-believe family."

Some sociologists compare the cults with "hippie" groups of the 1960s, with mysticism replacing drugs and religious devotion providing the sense of purpose once given by radical politics.

Still, some religious leaders find the authoritarianism in some cults "chilling," and are joining efforts to combat them.

One such leader, Rabbi Maurice Davis, has helped to organize a national network of groups composed of former cultists and parents of present members.

"Deprogramming" Efforts

Some parents in the last three years have resorted to abducting young people, usually by snatching them outside a commune, rushing them into a waiting car and speeding away.

Frequently, the youngster is turned over to a "deprogrammer" for four or five days of 20-hour-a-day "stressful interviewing" in a locked room, to rid the young person of cultist beliefs.

The best known of such deprogrammers, Ted Patrick, says that he has returned more than 1,000 "cured" believers to parents, although he admits his methods are illegal if the abducted cultist is past the legal age of adulthood....

Moves by Federal Government?

Signs of Federal Government involvement in the cult controversy are surfacing in Washington, D.C., where parental complaints of "psychological kidnaping" by cults have been coming into the U.S. Department of Justice at the rate of four or five a day.

Roger Cubbage, an attorney designated to handle these cases, says that Federal Bureau of Investigation agents are investigating two or three cult-related complaints a week. But he adds: "We've researched the law on coercion, and we simply can't find anything illegal in most of these allegations." ...

Religious scholars—and some parents too—suggest that cults may be socially beneficial to certain young people, considering the high rate of crime, suicide and other destructive behavior among youth today. Irving I. Zaretsky, coeditor of *Religious Movements in Contemporary America*, observes:

"Many entered cults to get free of drugs, and their rehabilitation rates are rather high, compared with government programs. What will happen if we cut off this relatively healthy outlet or antidote for antisocial behavior?"

Forecast: "Leveling Off"

How long will the present crop of cults continue to flourish? Martin E. Marty, of the University of Chicago Divinity School, sees signs that they may have peaked. "Campus leaders tell me the number of new recruits is leveling off, and most members leave after a few years in the cult," he says.

Professor Marty, a religious historian, predicts that none of today's cults will show the staying power of such dissenting faiths as the Jehovah's Witnesses and the Mormons.

As he sees it:

"Those groups were able to survive persecution and grow because they offered a structure of belief that would support people all through life and would encourage them to raise their children in the Church.

"But most of these cults are antagonistic toward nuclear families. They don't give their young members room to grow up."

THE JESUS CULT [3]

No one knows where, when, or how it began, but by 1967 there were traces of a reviving interest in Jesus among the "street people," "cop-outs," and "trippers" of California. Perhaps it began with "rock music"—a blend of jazz, blues, country and western and gospel music with a rhythmic beat of its own. The turning of "rock" to "protest" themes seemed to lead quite quickly to "secularized" religious themes to express and convey the message of disaffection and alienation. If this is true, it was no accident that gospel themes became more and more prominent, that even *Hair* had religious overtones, that *Jesus Christ Superstar* and *Godspel* had explicit Christian themes, and that "Amazing Grace" and "O Happy Day" should reach the top of the "hit parade." (By this time, of course, "Jesus rock" and "gospel music" had gone commercial and had become big business for the record companies and the disc jockeys.) For in contrast to neo-pentecostalism, the primary quest of the Jesus cult was "meaning" rather than "experience," although "experience" ran a close second to "meaning."

[3] From *Religion in America,* by Winthrop S. Hudson, professor of history, University of Rochester, and professor of history of Christianity, Rochester Center for Theological Studies. Scribner. '73. p. 431–3. Reprinted from *Religion in America,* 2nd edition by Winthrop S. Hudson with the permission of Charles Scribner's Sons. Copyright © 1965 Charles Scribner's Sons.

The new Christians among hippies, street people, and drug addicts quickly became known as Jesus Freaks, Jesus Trippers, Street Christians, or just plain Jesus People. It is difficult to generalize about them, for they were a variegated lot, having no common origin and frequently exhibiting intense hostility among themselves. One of the early groups arose in the Haight-Ashbury district of San Francisco as the result of the activity of Ted Wise, a sail maker from Sausalito, who was deeply involved in drug use. Late in 1967 his little group established a coffeehouse known as The Living Room, forerunner of a commune known as The House of Acts. Then one of the members, Lonnie Frisbee, felt called to Southern California where he founded a similar commune, The House of Miracles. Other members dispersed to New Knoxville, Ohio; Rye, New York; Eugene, Oregon; and Mill Valley, California, to extend the influence of the Jesus Way. Although the Jesus cult seems first to have flowered in California, a substantial segment of the movement appears to have originated in the Pacific Northwest, and similar spontaneous beginnings occurred elsewhere.

By 1970 there were Jesus groups everywhere, representing a surprisingly wide range of ideology. The Children of God, bluntly anti-establishment, legalistic, and authoritarian communalists, demanded a complete and disciplined separation (including forsaking and "hating" their parents) from the world which was soon to perish. In this respect, they were not greatly different from the Christian Foundation of Tony and Susan Alamo. Other groups were the products of free-lance evangelists, usually pentecostals, like Arthur Blessitt and Duane Pederson, both of whom forswore any connection with organized religion. Then there were groups that formed churches of their own and campus-oriented ministries such as the Christian World Liberation Front in Berkeley.

The appeal of Jesus to youth who had found organized religion apathetic and meaningless was not unlike the appeal of Oriental religions to some of their friends. With their pervading sense of emptiness and futility, they found in simple gospel texts meaning and direction which released them from drug-oriented escapes. And their new commitment, while not changing the life-style represented by dress and communes, did result in a shift to sober, disciplined living coupled with new excitement and purpose. While diverse, the Jesus people did tend to share some common emphases: an essentially nonintellectual insistence on the simple gospel; a strong belief that mankind was living in the last times; an espousal by some, but not all, of pentecostal gifts; a tendency toward communal living; an anti-institutional bias against organized Christianity; and a heavy dependence in their evangelism upon the hip language of "underground" newspapers and on music in the youth culture idiom.

It is difficult to assess how many were actually involved with the Jesus People. There was much coming and going. For some it was no more than the first step in going back home to Kansas, back to a more conventional life. But numbers were not as important as influence. As a result of widespread publicity, Jesus was definitely "in." He even became "commercial." And establishment organizations of a conservative bent, such as the Intervarsity Christian Fellowship and the Campus Crusade, were quick to capitalize on the new interest. The Intervarsity Fellowship assembled 12,000 students on the University of Illinois campus during the 1970 Christmas vacation ("Urbana '70")—a remarkable phenomenon at a time when conventional campus religious groups were dwindling. Equally impressive, although held at a more convenient time and more highly organized and financed, was Campus Crusade's "Explo '72" which brought 75,000 (mostly young people) to Dallas, Texas, in the summer of 1972. Many churches in all parts of the country began to feel the impetus that the Jesus movement had given their ministry to youth.

CULTS IN COURT [4]

A flurry of recent court cases suggests we are facing another test of how genuine our pluralism is and whether we will guarantee freedom of religion to movements that were not foreseen when the First Amendment was written.

Do the recruitment and training methods of the Hare Krishna sect constitute illegal mind control? A Queens [County, New York City] grand jury thinks so in the case of two individuals. But if the Krishna practices are illegal, what about the repetitious chanting and exclusion of family in [the] Trappist and Carthusian [orders of Catholicism?]. . . .

The courts, when they cannot avoid a decision, turn to some vague "man-in-the-street" idea of what "religion" should be: It involves prayer, and has something to do with a deity, etc. But a man-in-the-street approach would surely have ruled out early Christianity, which seemed both subversive and atheistic to the religious Romans of the day. The truth is that one man's "bizarre cult" is another's true path to salvation, and the Bill of Rights was designed to safeguard minorities from the man-on-the-street's uncertain capacity for tolerance.

The new challenge to our pluralism often comes from Oriental religious movements, because their views of religion differ so fundamentally from ours.

Oriental thought does not make our Western distinction between "science" and "religion," but sees a unified cosmos. Consequently, when the Transcendental Meditation organization designed a "Creative Intelligence" course for the New Jersey school system, the course was contested as a violation of the separation of church and state.

Eastern spirituality does not always make a clear distinction between religious and other types of behavior. This makes the legal situation more complex, since the tradi-

[4] From "Playing the Devil's Advocate, as It Were," by Harvey Cox, theologian and author, Victor Thomas Professor, Harvard Divinity School. New York *Times.* p A 25. F. 16, '77. © 1977 by the New York Times Company. Reprinted by permission.

tional focus of our thinking on this subject has been on institutions, not persons. The result has been chaotic, even for home-grown religious minorities.

By deciding on the limits of religious freedom, the courts have also been setting the perimeters of allowable personal behavior. But, again, they have been doing so, albeit inexplicitly, on the basis of an ethic derived from one religious tradition. Although Mormons have adjusted to monogamy, some of the newer movements encourage personal religious practices that run counter to current taboos. Should the courts deny freedom of expression in personal behavior because it goes against standards derived from a more familiar religion?

Some Oriental religious movements bother us because they pose a threat to the values of career success, individual competition, personal ambition and consumption, on which our economic system depends. We forget that Christianity, taken literally, could cause similar disquietude. Some psychiatrists contend that young people who join Oriental religious movements or Jesus communes have obviously been "brainwashed," since they now share their money and have lost interest in becoming successful executives. That someone could freely choose a path of mystical devotion, self-sacrifice and the sharing of worldly goods seems self-evidently impossible to them. They forget that these "crazy" attitudes have also been taught by St. Francis and . . . Baal Shem Tov [Jewish founder of modern Hasidism].

Indeed, according to the Gospel of Mark, Jesus was a candidate for "deprogramming," since his own family thought he was berserk and his religious leaders said he was possessed of the devil. One can sympathize with the sadness of parents whose offspring choose another way. But surely the rights of adults so to choose must be safeguarded if the First Amendment means anything.

My real fear about new religious movements is not that harassment will drive them out of existence, but rather that it could push them into premature accommodation, and we would lose the critical perspective that religion can bring to a culture in need of renewal.

Some new religious groups answer the need young people feel today for a way of life not based on accumulation and competition. Others promise an experience of the holy, undiluted by the accommodations Christianity and Judaism have made to consumer culture. Thus, minority religious movements can also be seen as symptoms of a hunger seemingly too deep for our existing religious institutions to feed.

I doubt if many people will ultimately find answers in these movements. Most of those who try an Oriental path will eventually find it too exotic for the Western psyche. They will then turn, as some are doing already, to the neglected spiritual and critical dimensions of our own traditions. Meanwhile, minority movements need protection, in part because they help us to see what is missing in our own way of life.

American culture has an enormous capacity to domesticate its critics. It is not unique in that respect. Christianity was once an exotic cult, providing a way of life visibly different from the jaded society around it. After a short period of persecution, it accommodated to the culture so well it was eventually accepted as Rome's only legitimate religion. Christians then quickly turned to the persecution of other religions. The same thing could happen to today's "cultists."

A new test of America's capacity for genuine pluralism is under way. We could flunk it by driving unconventional religious movements into accommodation before their message can be heard. I hope not. It is important to preserve freedom of religion, not only for the sake of the minority immediately involved but also because the majority needs to hear what the minority is saying.

VI. RELIGIOUS EDUCATION

EDITOR'S INTRODUCTION

The training of the young—not only *in* worship service but *through* various educational methods—is a part of virtually every religion. In the United States, the Constitution forbids any "established" religion, and religious training in the public schools systems is prohibited.

The first selection, from *U.S. News & World Report,* presents an overview of religious education in schools and in religious institutions themselves. S. Francis Overlan then examines the dilemma of Catholic parochial education.

A related topic is the 1962 and 1963 Supreme Court decisions barring prayer in public schools as unconstitutional. The next two selections present the background of these decisions and evidence that the issue is still a controversial one. In this section's final article, the Reverend John H. Krahn distinguishes between the overt religious practices barred by the Supreme Court rulings and the opportunities that still exist for learning about religion in the public schools.

RELIGION IN THE SCHOOLS [1]

Reprinted from *U.S. News & World Report.*

Church leaders, educators and parents nationwide are waging an uphill struggle to bring to U.S. youngsters a new interest in religion—and with it, more appreciation of traditional values and morality.

Arrayed against them in the aftermath of the 1960s youth revolt are hard facts: "religious illiteracy" among

[1] From "Comeback for Religion in Schools?" *U.S. News & World Report.* 79:53-6. Ag. 18, '75.

the young, declining enrollments in religious instruction in recent years, and court-decreed curbs on religious teachings or observances in public schools. [See "The School Prayer: I" and "The School Prayer: II," in this section, below.]

Further obstacles are seen in the soaring divorce rate and lack of parental guidance—prompting many church leaders to aim religious education at the entire family.

Even so—

More than at any time in recent years, churchmen find children and teen-agers today willing to accept religious instruction if it is imaginative and gives them a chance to participate.

Hundreds of public schools are offering study in comparative religion, Bible literature and other courses that show religion's role in history and culture.

More and more American college students are majoring in religious studies. States such as California, Michigan and Wisconsin are certifying public-school teachers to specialize in that field. . . .

In this uphill climb, resources are far from ample.

Despite renewed interest of parents in parochial schools, which seem to offer more discipline and more sharply defined values, such school systems continue to close because of the cost squeeze. Most families are forced to rely on traditional, church-centered religious education—the Sunday schools, the Jewish supplementary schools and the Catholic Confraternity of Christian Doctrine.

Yet progress is being made, church leaders feel.

Public Schools: Stressing Objective Religious Study

Courses about religion are among the most popular high-school electives. A survey by the National Council of Teachers of English shows that "Bible and literature" ranked in the top 10 of 180 commonly offered English courses.

Estimates are that about 1,000 public high schools give courses about religion. Many others are offering minicourses within regular classes in literature, history or social studies.

One expert predicts that, within the next decade, every public high school will offer such courses. About 50 per cent of elementary schools are said to be already including some form of objective study of religion.

Numerous new textbooks on religion are also being introduced. These texts, often commissioned by State education departments, are being designed for students from the early primary grades through college.

Colleges are preparing an increasing number of students to teach religious studies. At the University of California, Santa Barbara, about 300 students are majoring in that field.

The Public Education Religious Studies Center at Wright State University in Dayton, Ohio, conducts workshops and conferences, serves as a resource facility for curriculum development and provides a base for scholars of religion.

James Uphoff, who helped establish the center, says that even parochial schools seek assistance from the facility in order to design more well-rounded religion programs.

Mr. Uphoff explains that the purpose of religion courses in the public schools is not to indoctrinate students but simply to show what religion has done for man. He points out that, while the Supreme Court in 1963 ruled out Bible reading in schools, it affirmed the right to offer an objective study of religion.

At that time, Justice Tom Clark wrote: "One's education is not complete without a study of comparative religion or the history of religion and its relationship to the advancement of civilization. It certainly may be said that the Bible is worthy of study for its literary and historic qualities."

However, many school administrators are still uncertain about the meaning of the Court ruling and are leery about introducing courses on religion. . . .

Some educators are urging that schools include courses in ethics.

The Rev. James R. Blanning, director of the Council for Religion in Independent Schools, has developed a series of ethics cases now being used in a growing number of private and public high schools.

These cases, which are not linked to religious doctrines, give students a chance to explore their opinions on situations involving stealing, cheating or sexual relationships.

"In many cases, young people have had no religious instruction or come from homes where they receive little training in values," says Mr. Blanning. "By default, the school ends up being the purveyor of values and the rule maker, but it's usually ill-prepared.". . .

Parochial Schools: New Interest
Could Spark a Revival

Many parents are skeptical that the public schools can do much to deal with this problem.

Anna Gaumer, a teacher's aide in a Richmond, Calif., public school, says children can't get sufficient moral instruction in public schools, because teachers aren't given the time or leeway to treat such matters. She adds that children come from such varied backgrounds that efforts to teach ethics are very difficult.

Angelo Tramantano of Santa Monica, Calif., has transferred his children from a public to a parochial school, where he says "they're much happier and are getting religious teaching and discipline."

An Atlanta parent who made a similar switch says he sees a big improvement in his son's behavior.

In Cleveland, Mrs. Gene Isom, a Baptist, is sending her son to a Catholic school in the inner city, because "we like how our child is taught values."

Others, however, believe that the public schools often provide a more well-rounded education—and that the family's religious and moral training can offset the lack of such instruction in the schools. Says one Catholic parent in New York, who sends her children to public schools:

"It's much healthier for children to grow up learning to live with people of other religions. When you're in a Catholic school, you all go down the merry path together."

Such thinking, along with rising costs, has led to the closing of hundreds of Catholic schools. Enrollment in Catholic elementary and secondary schools has dropped from a peak of 5.7 million in 1964 to 3.5 million today. Catholic schools are also attracting an increasing number of minority students as white families move to the suburbs.

But the decline in enrollment may be ending. A National Opinion Research Center survey shows that 80 per cent of adult Catholics, including those without school-age children, would give more money each year to keep the local parochial school open.

Robert L. Lamborn, executive director of the Council for American Private Education, points to modest enrollment gains in most non-Catholic parochial schools. He explains:

"Although many parochial schools are struggling financially, there's still a willingness on the part of many families to make sacrifices so their children can get a value-oriented education."

Together, private schools now educate almost one tenth of America's 50.5 million elementary and secondary students.

Observers note a tremendous growth in the small parochial schools supported by fundamentalist denominations such as the Baptist Church and the Assembly of God. These schools now number much more than 5,000.

Many faiths are also putting more emphasis on education at the secondary level. Since 1959, there's been a 75 per cent increase in the number of students attending Jewish high schools, according to the American Association for Jewish Education. High-school students now make up about 20 per cent of the 82,000 enrolled in all-day Jewish schools. Another 400,000 attend afternoon or weekend sessions.

Rabbi Bernard Goldenberg of the National Society for Hebrew Day Schools reports that many parents regret not getting a strong-enough Jewish education and now want it for their children. Even Reform Jews, who previously sent their children to the public schools, are now opening new all-day facilities.

Albert Senske, education secretary for the Lutheran Church-Missouri Synod, which is opening five new high schools this year, adds that teen-agers are looking for more discipline and guidance and that private schools are best equipped to answer this need. Lutherans operate more schools than any other Protestant denomination.

At the college level, many religious-affiliated schools have de-emphasized required courses in theology.

Instead, they're offering a much wider range of elective courses in religion, often linked to student projects with the poor or other needy groups.

Outside the Schools: A Search for More Creative Programs

Most of the nation's young have no exposure to intensive religious instruction. For them, the major alternative is after-school or Sunday sessions.

The traditional Sunday school—at least among the mainline Protestant churches—has suffered huge drops in attendance in recent years, reports Elmer L. Towns, director of the Sunday School Research Institute in Savannah, Ga. He notes that 80 of the 100 largest Sunday schools are operated by small, evangelistic churches.

John H. Westerhoff III, associate professor of religion and education at Duke University Divinity School, traces this drop in interest to the increasing control that major churches exert over Sunday-school programs.

"Religious educators wanted to make Sunday school a formal school, with sophisticated texts and curriculum," he explains. "In doing so, they've destroyed many of the schools, because they've gotten away from the people and worship."

Some churches are putting a great deal of money and effort into changing this picture.

Fifteen Protestant denominations are now working on a 3.5-million-dollar project, called the Joint Educational Development program, designed to help churches create better Sunday-school programs—while still leaving control with the individual churches.

The Catholic Church, too, is investing the bulk of its religious-education resources into programs that take place outside of parochial schools. Many parishes now have a professional religious-education director, often a layman, and many of the 3,000 Catholic schools that were closed have been turned into religious-education centers.

Nearly all denominations have moved away from use of a formal text presenting a faith's major doctrines. Special committees have also been set up to eliminate disrespectful references to other religions in educational materials. Rabbi Marc Tanenbaum, director of inter-religious affairs for the American Jewish Committee, notes that religious-education courses now give more weight to the contributions of other faiths.

Now, most religious-education classes use a wide variety of instructional aids, plus group discussion and "sociodrama"—acting out problem situations. The focus is on the child's personal needs and the kinds of information he's interested in. Civic and world affairs are also stressed. . . .

Some churches—both Protestant and Catholic—are going beyond the classroom to reach young people. They've set up "youth ministry" programs in which young adults give a year or two, full time, to working with teens and getting them into counseling, recreational and religious programs.

In St. Paul, Minn., Roger Beaubien of the Catholic Education Center estimates that each youth minister makes close contact with 300 teen-agers each year. Most of these young people are those who refused religious instruction.

Similarly, the Mormon Church reports continuing success with its missionary program in which youths give two years to evangelistic work. Bishop Burke Peterson of Salt

Lake City says young people are enthusiastic about the church because they've been given a big role.

Church camping continues to grow, says the Rev. Rodney Young, assistant program director of the Council of Churches of Greater Washington. He sees camping as a way for children to learn from the example of respected leaders.

What all this means is that churches doubt the effectiveness of the old one or two-hour weekly religion classes.

That approach worked well, educators say, when families lived in close-knit neighborhoods and communities that supported their beliefs. Now, especially in suburbs, experts believe more time is needed to build a church community.

Some churches take advantage of released time that certain public schools give to students for activities at church centers. In St. Paul, high-school students spend one full day of released time each month at the Catholic Education Center. Director Roger Beaubien says the concept offers the chance to design more intensive and creative activities. Attendance is nearly 95 per cent.

Churches are also trying to join adults with children and teen-agers in retreats, summer conferences and many other activities besides worship.

And increasingly, adult education is being stressed to get parents involved more in the moral development of their children. The Lutheran Church is now conducting a parent effectiveness-training program for thousands of its members.

Says the Rev. John Harvey, a Catholic religious-education teacher in Hays, Kans.: "We can teach all day long, but everything comes undone if the parent's behavior contradicts it all."

Baptist theologian Carl F. H. Henry believes that young people are more interested in religion now. Mr. Henry sees the appeal of materialism and secularism as fading and insists that America's churches have a "golden opportunity" to fill the vacuum.

DECLINE OF CATHOLIC PAROCHIAL SCHOOLS [2]

The most widely expressed and believed explanation of declining enrollments in Catholic schools centers on financing. This theory observes that it does, indeed, cost more today than yesterday to keep Catholic schools open. Throughout this century, Catholic schools have been endowed by the cheap labor of nuns, brothers and priests—much as private nonsectarian prep schools of the Northeast have been endowed by gifts from wealthy alumni. When the number of religious vocations dwindled, the number of lay teachers increased. The latter began to demand salaries somewhat comparable to their public school colleagues; the cost (although not always the price) of Catholic schooling rose accordingly.

A variant of this death-by-economics argument—not so widely touted—emphasizes the monopolistic character of public schooling. This theory holds that, since school costs a lot of money, and since the government controls about 90 percent of the nation's elementary and secondary school market, the actions of the public monopoly profoundly affect the existence of private schools. In the decade between 1962 and 1972, for example, the per pupil cost of public education in the United States rose by almost 140 percent. This means that parents wishing to send their children to Catholic or other nonpublic schools had first to pay their share of soaring public school costs, leaving themselves strapped for private educational expenditures. If things continue through the 1970s along the path established in the 1960s, only the very, very affluent who can afford higher taxes and then heavier private school tuitions will be able to exercise their constitutional right to choose private education.

Probably the next most widely cherished explanation for the death of parochial schooling focuses on lack of demand. A favorite stance of Catholic traditionalists appears to be

[2] From "Why Are Parochial Schools Closing?" by S. Francis Overlan, director, Education Voucher Project, Center for the Study of Public Policy. *America.* 131:111–13. S. 14, '74. Reprinted with permission of *America* 1974. All rights reserved. © 1974 by America Press, 106 W. 56th Street, New York, NY 10019.

that espoused by Msgr. [Michael] McGuire: "The attendance decline in parochial schools is in large measure due to the unwholesome teaching of religion therein." There should be no mistake about it. The monsignor does not believe that the teaching of religion in Catholic schools is "unwholesome" in the way that, say, Americans United for Separation of Church and State might. For he continues: "Thousands of parents have withdrawn their children because the faith of our fathers is not being taught by many extremely progressive religious and lay teachers." This statement rests on the conviction that American Catholic parents are devaluing parochial education because that kind of schooling is becoming more progressive and less Catholic.

A fundamentally similar explanation for the decline of attendance in Catholic schools is contradictory in detail. It traces the meteoric rise of the faithful up the nation's socioeconomic ladder. And it contends that, in the process of becoming successful Americans, Catholics have felt less need for their ghetto, a need earlier expressed by a desire for separate schools. This hypothesis depends on a number of assumptions, including some or all of the following: 1) that American Catholics feel that they can take care of religious training either within the family or with the sporadic help of CCD [Confraternity of Christian Doctrine] or CYO [Catholic Youth Organization]; 2) that American Catholics are coming to place a higher value on secular education than on religious learning; 3) that American Catholics believe that secular teaching is better done in public schools.

Another explanation for dwindling parochial school enrollment appears less complex. It holds that there are fewer Catholic children and, therefore, a smaller pool of potential students. Ultimately, of course, this raises questions about the cause of the declining American Catholic birthrate. To the extent that "the pill" is a factor, and to the extent that the pill is prescribed by the improved socioeconomic status of American Catholics, this explanation of declining enrollments is simply a cousin (once removed) of the lack-of-demand theory described above.

Yet another hypothesis in this partial list blames the clergy for Catholic school closings. Their management of the complex and expensive system of parochial education, so this argument goes, can only be described as bungling. For example, they are accused of putting too much political muscle behind the abortion issue when more should have been applied to aid for parochial schools. Others charge that ecclesiastics failed to build enough schools in the suburbs as Catholics migrated there. In sum, this hypothesis sees the clerical administrators of parochial schools as unwitting accomplices in the demise of formal Catholic schooling.

A more recent explanation for the decline in Catholic school enrollment is that developed by Fr. [Andrew] Greeley, who heads the Center for the Study of American Pluralism at the University of Chicago's National Opinion Research Center. . . . "Catholic schools," he writes, "will go out of existence mostly because Catholic educators no longer have enough confidence in what they are doing to sustain the momentum and the sacrifice that built the world's largest private school system." By implication, Fr. Greeley recommends self-assurance for parochial school employees and managers—an antidote he hopes will be effective and contagious.

Of course, one can with equal conviction devise plausible explanations in addition to those above for the dramatic decline in Catholic school enrollments. One of my pet theories takes a novel view of the operations of the public school monopoly. According to this view, the fact that approximately 90 percent of America's elementary and secondary students attend public schools results not from a sinister economic force that eliminates its private competition, but from an attractive and gentle monopoly of our minds. This theory attempts to explain the continued vitality and the vigorous growth of public enrollments rather than the decline of Catholic (or, for that matter,

noncoeducational or military) enrollments. The positing of
a responsive and satisfying public monopoly of education
explains why so many wealthy WASPs—who could have
afforded elite private schools for their children—have so
long and so overwhelmingly patronized public institutions.
And it explains why so many Catholic parents—both poor
and middle class—have contentedly sent their children to
public schools even before the crisis in Catholic enrollments
began. It also provides insight into the imitative behavior
of Catholic schools during the last decade or so, as they
dropped class sizes and reformed curriculum, thereby making them more like the public counterparts.

Curiously enough, this attraction to the ways of public
educationists probably contributed mightily to increased
costs for Catholic schooling. The financial outcome makes
one believe that a harsh economic monopoly is at work. In
fact, however, the effective monopoly is a psychological one.
It is important to make the distinction. For, if one wanted
to take remedial action against a monopoly, one might
attack the psychological monopoly differently from the
economic.

The foregoing, even with a new theory added, is an
incomplete list of explanations for Catholic school closings.
There are more, and probably others will be developed as
the crisis continues. All of this leads to an inevitable question: Are there not too many explanations for the impend-
ing death of Catholic schools?

Any pragmatist determined to save Catholic schooling
would recommend answering in the affirmative. For, if
beset with so many diseases, Catholic schools are surely
doomed. The crisis looks too complex to be solved. It may
simply be, however, that too little diagnostic skill has been
applied to defining the real cause—or the few most important causes—of enrollment declines. By reasonable laws
of evidence, some explanations must be eliminated. The
remainder must certainly be classified on a scale from
critical to trivial. Such an approach is justified by the
observation that some of the explanations, when combined,

lead to apparent contradictions. For example, how can the implied solution that Catholic schools must be made more "traditional" be melded with the implied solution that Catholic schools must become more "progressive"?

This pragmatic approach is bolstered by the further observation that the number and apparent contrariness of the explanations reveal the hidden hand of self-protective partisanship. Liberal Catholics find that money is not the basic problem, but that Catholic schools spend too much time on Père Marquette and too little on world population problems. Curious that their conclusions conform to their earlier convictions. Traditional Catholics conclude that the problem of dwindling enrollments results from loss of contact with the faith of their fathers. This finding, of course, coincides with their expectations. Ecclesiastics discover that the root of the evil is money. Curious, too, that such a conclusion need not require a reexamination of Catholic life and values in America in relation to Catholic schools in America. Quite by accident, everyone arrives at a comfortable conclusion—at least for his camp!

THE SCHOOL PRAYER RULINGS: I [3]

Few, if any, controversies of the present era have remained so persistently before the U.S. Congress as has that over the 1962 and 1963 Supreme Court rulings which declared unconstitutional prayer and Bible reading conducted under government auspices in public schools. Over the years since 1963, every Congress has seen the introduction of proposals seeking, by amending the U.S. Constitution—most commonly by expressly authorizing some form of "voluntary" prayer—to nullify the effects of the Court's decisions.

Throughout this period, Congress has been the target of an intensive lobbying effort, both on the part of those pressing for a "prayer amendment" and by those opposing

[3] From foreword to "Congress and the 'School Prayer' Controversy." *Congressional Digest*. 53:3. Ja. '74. Reprinted by permission.

any modification of the present First Amendment language affecting church-state relations. Initially, the extensive hearings held before the Judiciary Committee of the House of Representatives in 1964 served, momentarily at least, as a "pressure valve" for the strong public feeling which had built up on both sides of the controversy. However, no action took place at that time beyond the printing of the voluminous hearing record.

Since that time, the continuation of an organized effort by individuals and groups promoting the prayer amendment approach, hearings in the Senate in 1966, an unsuccessful effort for approval of an amendment in 1971 in the House of Representatives, and a renewal of Senate consideration of the subject in the present 93rd Congress all have tended to keep alive the emotionally-charged "school prayer" controversy.

Actually, "school prayer" has become a term of convenience used to refer to a variety of public practices with religious connotations, including not only prayer and Bible reading in public places but references to a Supreme Being in public oaths and patriotic creeds, the appearance of the motto "In God we trust" on U.S. coinage, and a variety of other practices long regarded as a part of the American heritage. In the aftermath of the original landmark decisions of the Supreme Court have come a number of other Federal and State court rulings involving religion-related subject areas such as those enumerated above.

A major consequence has been confusion among much of the U.S. public over what the Supreme Court did and did not say, as well as a frequently-expressed feeling that the Court may have ventured into an area not properly a subject for judicial process.

In the decade which has ensued since the school prayer controversy first erupted, a few nationally significant groups prominent in the controversy have modified their positions. But by and large, both the alignment of organizations and interests, and the arguments brought to bear for and against the proposition of a prayer amendment to the Constitution, have remained substantially unchanged.

Notwithstanding the familiarity of its arguments, however, the school prayer controversy is legislatively a highly complex one—involving a long body of practice and tradition, interpretation of the intentions of the Founding Fathers, and a series of court decisions, themselves often less than totally clear. It is also, as any analysis of the decade-long debate reveals, a highly emotional subject.

Thus Congress, in once again grappling with the question of what to do about "school prayer," must not only weigh the long-range implications for American society of modifying the Constitution's First Amendment, but must also respond to continuing evidence that, regardless of the legal niceties involved in the controversy, the events and changes brought about by the original Supreme Court "prayer" decisions still are seen by many—more than ten years after the fact—as "just not right."

With such considerations remaining prominent . . . , the fate of "school prayer" . . . remains difficult to foresee.

THE SCHOOL PRAYER RULINGS: II [4]

Reprinted from *U.S. News & World Report.*

More than a decade after the Supreme Court banned prescribed prayers and Bible reading in public schools, a new push is on to restore such activities to the classroom.

Two States—New Hampshire and Connecticut—recently passed laws allowing voluntary, nondenominational prayer.

Other State legislatures are considering similar bills. And in some parts of the nation, school prayer continues—in open defiance of the Court ruling.

Voluntary Prayer

The New Hampshire law permits local school boards to authorize voluntary recitation of the Lord's Prayer.

[4] From "Prayer in Schools—Still a Troubling Problem." *U.S. News & World Report.* 79:56. Ag. 18, '75.

Students not wishing to take part can excuse themselves. . . .

The Connecticut law requires local school boards to set aside a period each day for "silent meditation." Massachusetts passed a similar law in 1973. Texas and New Jersey have also been considering such a measure.

In Ohio, too, teachers are allowed to set aside time for meditation on moral or patriotic themes.

Critics, however, feel that meditation is just another word for prayer in many instances and should be ruled unconstitutional. . . .

Some school districts have ignored the ban. A survey by R. B. Dierenfield of Macalester College in St. Paul, Minn., shows that nearly half of the school districts in the South conduct Bible readings and other devotions. . . .

Chances are . . . considered to be slim for a constitutional amendment guaranteeing the right of school prayer. . . .

Lawmakers who advocate the amendments—mostly from rural areas—say there's strong support for school prayer. But opponents balk at another change in the First Amendment, which provides for separation of church and state and guarantees freedom of religion.

RELIGION AS PART OF GENERAL STUDIES [5]

Most teachers view their pupils in a limited way and do not get involved with religious concerns. Yet their students' ultimate concerns will not go away, will not stop being ultimate, will not stop having profound implications in their daily lives. Lack of involvement in ultimate concerns is the result of a particular set of circumstances in part historical, in part educational, and in part personal. The public school is ofen weakest at a point where its potential for significant and exciting discovery is greatest. At least four factors help account for neglect in this area.

[5] From "Religion: An Integral Part of Public Education," by John H. Krahn, pastor, Trinity Lutheran Church, Hicksville, New York. *Clearing House.* 48:356-60. F. '74. Reprinted by permission.

The first factor is the much misunderstood, recent court decisions concerning the practice of religion in public schools. It has become a "hot potato" and many teachers have chosen to ignore it rather than discover the boundaries in which the study about religion can be legally pursued.

A second factor is that the scientific methodology of behavior modification and similar models of teaching in vogue today militate against a humanistic approach to man. Mental processes are considered paramount. Human behavior is shaped into desired patterns through operant conditioning. Man is controlled through positive rewards. In practice there seems to be no place for a Martin Buber [Jewish philosopher] and his suggestion that we encounter a fellow human being as something much more than a means to an end. Buber's suggestion in *I and Thou* that we stand in relation to another You as a whole being comprised of much more than the sum total of its parts is not appreciated. Instead, all of life is relegated to the dehumanizing I-It relationship, losing the beautiful experience of the reciprocity of another You.

A third consideration is that religion is an area in which teachers have been poorly trained. They have felt inadequate and have consequently avoided the subject.

The fourth factor is perhaps the strongest deterrent. Many teachers find it difficult to consider ultimate concerns and have therefore avoided them. There has been little personal integration. When a student asks a question or the subject flows naturally from some reading or event, the teacher is not emotionally prepared to handle it. He therefore avoids or glosses over it.

Although these four factors are understandable, they are not acceptable. As man develops, his intellect is only one of many areas which needs to be nurtured. Other areas commonly delineated include his social, aesthetic, moral, psychological, physical, and spiritual nature. These qualities of humanity must not be neglected.

The Anisa Model

There are some educators who feel that man's spiritual nature should be the core of the educational experience. Daniel C. Jordan of the Center for the Study of Human Potential at the School of Education of the University of Massachusetts in Amherst feels that a new educational system must be organized around an affirmation of the spiritual nature of man. . . . This new educational model is called *Anisa* from an Arabic word meaning "a tree in a high place that sheds a fragrance all around"—the Tree of Life, symbolizing continual growth and fruitation.

The Anisa Model redefines education as those processes or experiences which release man's human potential. It rests on the bold assertion that man is "the pinnacle of creation, endowed with unique capacities still unfathomed and for the most part unrealized."

Affirming the spiritual nature of man, Anisa encourages the development of his infinite potentialities for both his good and that of his fellowman. Man's spiritual nature serves as the unifying principle for the Anisa Model on the philosophical level. On the functional level knowing and loving are the two basic capacities of man which reflect his purpose. The interplay of these two capacities produce positive and creative action. . . .

Many school districts throughout the country have curricular units on the Bible as Literature and on Comparative Religions. In most cases these curricular materials avoid encouraging the practice of a particular religion. There are some exceptions. In the "Curriculum Guide for the Teaching of Bible" in the public schools of North Carolina, revised 1965, some of the objectives include: "to guide the child in worship experiences, to help the child find in his study of the Bible a personal relationship with Jesus Christ as his Savior, Lord, Leader and Friend, to help the child find in his study of the Bible answers to the great questions . . . such as the meaning of God, Life, Sin and Death." Obviously this is in violation of the Supreme Court's ruling.

Many school districts handle religious education through programs of released time worked out in conjunction with local churches. In New York State one hour of school time per week can be allotted for released time.

At Harriton High School in Rosemont, Pennsylvania, there is a very interesting approach to religious education. Religious leaders in the community are invited to teach a unit on Religion. In a recent unit 15 speakers running the gamut from a representative of . . . Ethical Culture to a major from the Salvation Army took part. Evaluation of the course was filled with plaudits [such as] "We've experienced four weeks that we'll never forget." Most of the students and faculty were impressed by the sincerity and dignity of the "Men of God" who participated. . . .

Two Levels of Approach

There are two levels on which religion can be approached in the public school. Both are valid and useful but for different reasons. Both have been alluded to in this article. The first level I will call the objective approach level and the second the subjective approach level. The first deals with form, the second with substance.

Using the objective approach, Sacred Scripture is read and studied as a literature characteristic of certain periods in history. Literary types (epic, rhetoric, wisdom, lyric, prophetic) can be extracted and studied. Beliefs can be viewed in relation to culture. Characteristics of various beliefs can be compared. All is educationally sound and defensible. Yet man's ultimate concerns need not be considered when using this approach.

More important for our discussion is the subjective approach level. On this deeper level ultimate concerns are discussed and integrated. Children are encouraged to react to themes of origin, life, and death, which pervade all of religious literature.

Great literature and the arts are other areas in which the ultimate concerns are consistently encountered. . . . The arts constantly encounter life at every level. There is no drama without reaching for the boundaries of human existence. The arts provide much opportunity for meaningful encounter on the subjective approach level to religion. Existential involvement is encouraged. Group discussion should occur.

The relatively new encounter model of teaching might very well facilitate such existential interaction. Using this model and its techniques to "open up" discussion, children in small groups share their experiences and feelings about ultimate concerns and commitments. Each child is encouraged to explain his "gut" feelings and then to identify as much as possible with the feelings of others. . . .

Religion must be subjective to be experienced. Subjectivity is integral to the "discipline," and therefore must be encouraged. Even such subjectivity is allowable in public education as long as it is approached objectively. In other words each student's subjective approach to ultimate concerns must be allowed. His spiritual insights are encouraged. Prescribing one's subjectivity over another's is not permitted. Objective subjectivity comes from affirming everyone's subjectivity.

VII. A VIEW TO THE FUTURE

EDITOR'S INTRODUCTION

It is doubtful that, twenty years ago, it would have been reasonable to predict the religious resurgence and turmoil that have been the subject of this volume. Predictions as to the future are equally difficult. General economic prosperity or hardship, a world atmosphere of peace or hostility—these and other factors will all have their influence.

Whether today's heightened interest in religion is the beginning of a long-range trend or merely a fad is difficult to foretell, but in this section some predictions are hazarded. First, there is a look at the future of the "organized and traditional" religions. A consideration of the future of the "new" religious movements follows. In conclusion, two selections take up the topic of church unification and the potential for greater harmony among America's multitude of faiths.

CHOICES FOR THE ESTABLISHED RELIGIONS [1]

What about organized and traditional religions? When you examine them, you feel at first that they should be in for the best times. . . . The sting and hate is gone out of many relationships—or so it seems. . . . There are encouraging signs such as the Mormons weakening in their scriptural bias against blacks. And, obviously, we can stand an occasional fracas on the order of Leonard Bernstein's blasphemous treatment of Chalice and Sacrament in his so-called *Mass*, or the time-worn Jewish stereotypes trotted out fecklessly in *Jesus Christ Superstar*.

[1] From "Religion: All Quiet on the Western Front," by Malachi B. Martin, writer on religion and formerly a Jesuit professor at the Pontifical Biblical Institute in Rome. *National Review.* 26:926—8. Ag. 16, '74. Reprinted by permission of National Review, 150 East 35th Street, New York, New York 10016, subscription $19 per year.

Furthermore, there is the quite amicable give-and-take of ecumenism in the afterglow of the Second Vatican Council [as] Protestants and Catholics, and sometimes even Jews, exchange pulpits. Catholic and Rabbinic authorities have a smooth understanding about points of former friction (e.g., mixed marriages, co-celebration of funerals, etc.). Catholics, Jews, and Protestants partake of social activism together, and are particularly united in political activism (the Clergy and Laity Concerned with Vietnam and joint resolutions on Watergate are just two of many good examples). The steady Protestantization of Catholics after the Vatican Council and the Romanization of many of the larger Protestant denominations have been supplemented by formal talks between some of them which bid fair to ease doctrinal differences by smoothing sharply worded terminology and by expanding precise formularies to acceptably general and noncommittal statements of agreement. At least, people are trying to be agreeable.

Bureaucracy and Go-Go

But, on close examination, most major religious denominations seem to suffer from one or both of two major afflictions. There is either a general paralysis in religious leadership that must be counted as bulking large in the increasing ineffectualness of religion in this troubled environment of ours. Or there is a behaviorism. . . .

The paralysis in leadership only allows of ecclesiastical bureaucracy with its mainstays: committees, blueprints, political influence, democratizing discussions, job-hunting and patronage, managerial projections, and the anonymous gravamen of any bureaucratic body whose chief aim must be self-preservation. Add to this a brutal fact of life today: to survive physically within an economy as inflationary as ours, organizations must devote 85 per cent of their energies to active concern with economic viability. Men concerned mainly with money and economic viability are the same all over the world. There is nothing specifically religious about them.

The second affliction, the behaviorism, is quite another thing. It bursts forth unexpectedly—kaleidoscopic, gyrating, fleeting, changing. It is everywhere, anywhere, every day. Are you in the mood for comic relief? Take Shirley Thomas, professional exotic dancer in a coin-covered bikini, knocking out a go-go dance to the strains of the Beatles' "Money," while they pass the plate in the Unitarian Universalist Congregational Church of Atlanta. Are you looking for the illogical and the irrelevant? Listen to [biblical historian] G. Wilson Knight asserting that Jesus was "androgynous, filled with both masculinity and femininity, thus transcending our sexuality while he shares it." The pathetic? Here is Betty Friedan speaking to the trenchantly phrased question "Is God He, or Was God He, or How Did That Come About?" at a New York Town Hall debate. Want to sample the pointless? Stop by for a really new Mass said on a living room sofa in suburban New Jersey. The irresponsible? Read Dan Berrigan likening his unlawful underground flight from the FBI to St. John's Dark Night of the Soul, and blink to see him later hailed as a man of conscience in a public statement released by major religious superiors. Care to weep? Witness Jean Cardinal Danielou's death in suspicious and painfully embarrassing circumstances, followed by no meaningful statement from his fellow Princes in the Church, only by an attempted coverup and the awkward and saddening silence we have come to expect from any ordinary power brokers dealing with their tainted image.

Whatever it may be, one must usually categorize the particular initiative as merely a religious imitation or an imitation by a religious person of some social, political, or cultural activity. Among the 200 rising leaders of our American future listed in the July 15 issue of *Time* magazine, there are six clergymen. Each one's claim to a place on that distinguished roster lies in the sphere of social activism (and no one can fault them in that) for which their clerical identities served as launching pads. None has given equally outstanding religious leadership. . . .

Those six clergymen, fairly chosen and duly representative, are almost a modern parable in themselves. For, apart
from a certain diminishing hard core in each of the major
Christian denominations as well as in the small (2 per cent
of the total population) Jewish sector, the bulk seems to be
undergoing total immersion in the ambience to the point
of having no specifically religious reaction, proposal, policy,
or interpretation of their own. . . .

[A] recent report of the National Conference of Catholic
Bishops is a belated official recognition of the resultant
dilemma. "Transcendent religious belief," it concludes,
"finds itself engaged in direct contestation with a secularistic and humanistic world view which rejects religion and
absolute moral values." Alas, such recognition is just a
mite too late. "Direct contestation" seems to be over. Our
religious organizations and religionists have for too long
had recourse primarily to secular power and its principles
of self-preservation. The "secularistic" and the "humanistic"
rejected the specifically religious some time ago; they have
conquered and been accepted in its place.

Now, some time after the event, even as all power is
mysteriously slipping away from the grasp of its traditional
possessors, religions and their institutions too are in the
same lurch as all centers of this-world power. It is not surprising. In the face of this stark reality so lately admitted,
the major Christian denominations (Anglican/Episcopal,
Roman Catholic, Eastern Orthodox) have a major and two-
faceted problem: can they cut loose from the company of
power brokers? And can they rely on spirit for authority?
Probably, they cannot. It is more than flesh and blood can
accept. And their efforts, in any case, seem to be to change
the bureaucracy, but to leave the soul as it is.

The lesser Christian denominations, afflicted by the same
power associations and drives, have an additional problem:
can they rid themselves of their idiosyncrasies and small
triumphalisms, to follow the spirt's urging, to fuse with
that spirit's work as it leavens the whole? Again, probably
not. Most of them would cease to exist as distinct entities.

And suicide (as they would consider it to be) is not palatable.

While Jewish religionists have to deal with thorny problems concerning the elite and race (both central to Judaism and, paradoxically, both unacceptable terms in today's climate), their principal problem is again related to power. For Judaism becomes (for many Jews) a humanistic attachment to an ancient cultural heritage centered in Israel. For many others, it becomes a supreme loyalty—overriding their present nationalisms—to a sociopolitical entity (Israel) as the only guarantee against "another Hitler and another holocaust." And in neither case, of course, are we talking of spirit, but of attachment to power in the material order. Will Judaism itself now turn to spirit for its religious reliance and inspiration? Probably not. The recent past is too traumatic. The near future is too problematic.

Part-Time Panic

As far as this writer is concerned, and with all these circumstances as a backdrop, there are chiefly two signposts to guide his analysis of, and commentary on, religion today. One is the evident breakup of institutions. The other —a more intangible one—is to be found in the emergent effects of spirit working within this human universe.

Very few of us now are not aware of the breakup. We realize that the cement between the building blocks of religious and civil institutions is crumbling, that the vital firmness in the traditional molds of our humanness is weakening. Hence, our part-time panic, our periodic pessimisms, and our bursts of febrile inventiveness to keep the whole thing going in the hope that the wind of change will die down. And, in spite of any well intentioned prophecy of round-the-corner Pentecostals, there is realistically nothing in view at present but an autumn deepening into winter, in which one can foresee only further dislocation, fragmentation, social anarchy, vain personalisms, confusions, diminishing liberties, and wild desire.

Looked upon with a materialist eye the situation calls, first, for purely social, psychological, and political explanations; and, consequently, for solutions exclusively deriving from such explanations. But, as we are already finding out, such solutions and explanations lead only to repetitions of past historical mistakes and, thence, to new or deepened crises. No traditional "mix" seems to work any more. All our solutions seem to be jinxed.

To the religious eye, the breakup is the effect of spirit in a universe that has been saved by gratuitous and eternal love. For that eye, reality dictates that only the dimension of spirit restored to our calculations will eventually see us through our winter.

The workings of the spirit are subtle and, because our modern mind is trained to unknow them, largely unrecognizable by us. We only recognize what we know. Religious commentary must discover the outlines of spirit by scrutinizing newly emergent conditions: negative ones, such as the disappearance of cultural presuppositions, regional bastions, parochial blindnesses, individual prejudices; positive ones, such as the several traits of a new inner commonality shared by greater and greater numbers of men and women all over the globe.

Chiefly, however, the commentator's gaze must be on organized religions of East and West today. For they are now confronted with a bare choice. Many religionists may take a long time to acknowledge it. They will either cooperate with that ruthless autumnal winnowing of the spirit and be purified of their reliance on material power during the long winter wait; or, with a strong dose of this-worldly realism, they will finally surrender even the thinnest pretense to be at spirit's disposal: they will reject the hope and promise of spirit, making their own that hideous equanimity of the ancient pagan buried on the Aventine in Rome whose tomb inscription is a summation of finality and the grinning antithesis of hope: *Hodie mihi, cras tibi* (I today, you tomorrow).

FUTURE OF NEW RELIGIOUS MOVEMENTS [2]

There are signs . . . across the country that the youth-oriented religious sects that sprang into existence a few years ago are gaining a foothold for an enduring future.

The emergence of a wide assortment of spiritual movements, from Eastern religions to "Jesus" people, has been the principal feature of a resurgence of interest in religion among America's young people. Many movements, demanding intensive commitment, have evoked strong criticism from parents and public officials who believe the freedom of group members may have been violated.

After nearly a decade of this ferment, the underlying question is whether these new groups will last. The answer appears to be that most of them, though faced with high attrition rates and continuing obstacles to survival, have retained a small but sufficient core of devoted followers and are acquiring the resources needed to continue their work.

Court Battles

Among the most significant indications of this preparation for the long haul is the increasing willingness of sect members to seek legitimacy for their religious commitment through the courts.

At least six lawsuits have been instigated against "deprogrammers" who removed followers from their sects and tried to dissuade them from returning. The plaintiffs include members of Hare Krishna, the Unification Church of Sun Myung Moon and The Way. . . .

"Feature of Profound Change"

The new religious groups are raising fundamental cultural and legal questions that are attracting growing attention from scholars.

[2] From "New Religious Movements Considered Likely to Last," by Kenneth A. Briggs, staff writer. New York *Times*. p A 15. Je. 22, '77. © 1977 The New York Times Company. Reprinted by permission.

"The new religious movement, in its broadest sense, can no longer be taken as a transitory cultural aberration," Professor Jacob Needleman of San Francisco State University said last week, "but rather as a central feature of the profound change through which the American civilization is now passing."

Dr. Needleman spoke at a national conference on the new movements, held at the Graduate Theological Union in Berkeley.

His view was shared by most of the 35 sociologists, theologians and journalists at the conference. One of the purposes of the four-day gathering was to muster support for a proposed center for the study of new religions at the Graduate Theological Union, a consortium of nine theological schools.

Goals of Research

The center would be the first of its kind in the United States, and could help provide information on the origins, growth and character of dozens of religious groups.

One of the principal aims of its research would be to sort out fact from popular fiction about such groups and to measure their impact on other institutions. Until now, scholars say, little has been learned about most of the sects, partly because they have only recently been seen as important cultural factors.

Academicians disagree as to how great that impact has been. But most who have studied the question concur that the groups signify deep longings for meaning and a search for a more satisfactory sense of self. They also appear to represent serious challenges to Western thought that have caused many people to turn away from material gain, competition and the success ethic.

Peace and Power

Professor Frederick Bird of Concordia University in Montreal, who has studied followers of new groups for several years, told the conference that their "appeal relates to the fact that participants find that ritual practice provides the self with a validating experience and self-protecting armor against the exigencies of internal and external threats."

Theodore Roszak, the historian and author, said he believed that the new movements reflected a deep desire for transcendence and posed critical opposition to modern secular humanism. The lesson taught by this "religious renaissance," Professor Roszak said, is that "we can use its conception of human potentiality to challenge the adequacy of our science, our . . . [techniques], our politics."

Those groups to whom these functions are ascribed represent a highly diverse variety of cults, meditation centers, rural communes, loosely organized associations and highly structured churches. However, if religion is defined as any cluster of values around which people shape their lives, a growing number of Americans appear to be taking part in one movement or another. . . .

Outsiders have shown by far the greatest concern about the high-intensity groups such as the Unification Church and Hare Krishna.

Preliminary studies of both groups, including the most extensive survey, by Professor Stillman Judah of the Graduate Theological Union, show a small core membership (about 3,000 in the case of the Unification Church) and a small though steady growth rate.

The dropout rate is high among these groups. Professor Judah and Professor Bird have both surveyed youth populations and discovered that of all those who had had some contact with a new religious movement only 25 percent were still involved. In Professor Judah's sample, 55 percent of those in the Bay area had been involved less than a year.

But through persistent evangelistic efforts, these groups are winning new converts and attaining fiscal stability. For example, according to Professor Judah, the Unification Church expects to discontinue street sales of candy and other items in three years, hoping to have become totally reliant upon businesses by then. And Hare Krishna is said to be planning a new incense factory in Mexico to supplement its businesses in this country.

If historical patterns prevail, even the most controversial movements may find greater acceptance in America's religious pluralism. Much the same process of harsh criticism and later toleration has followed such groups as the Mormons, Christian Scientists and Jehovah's Witnesses.

Religious Myths

But in the interim, said Harvey Cox, a Harvard theologian, many of these groups will bear the brunt of certain "myths" believed by the religious and cultural majority. Professor Cox identifies four such myths throughout history toward new groups: that they are subversive, that they encourage sexual perversion, that they refuse to tell the truth about themselves and that they employ means of duping followers.

The vigor and general acceptability of the new movements vary greatly. But whatever the response, scholars generally agree that the old and the new religions in this country have begun to influence each other and will continue to do so. To a degree out of proportion to their relatively small numbers, the groups are causing organized religion to do considerable thinking about their mission and purpose.

Professor Roszak said that the outcome of the struggle by new religions would be of immense consequence.

CONSULTATION ON CHURCH UNION [3]

Delegates to COCU's 1974 plenary session in Cincinnati were told by General Secretary Gerald Moede that the Consultation on Church Union is a "delicate flower, only beginning to push through the ground." But after 12 years of

[3] From "The 'Postdenominational' Church: Will COCU's 'Delicate Flower' Blossom?" by Paul M. Minus Jr., professor, church history, Methodist Theological School, Delaware, Ohio. *Christian Century*. 92:83–6. Ja. 29, '75. Copyright 1975 Christian Century Foundation. Reprinted by permission from the January 29, 1975 issue of *The Christian Century*.

waiting, one is entitled to ask if the fragile sprout will ever blossom.

There are reasons for doubt. The COCU agenda is ambitious and far-reaching, but COCU's staff and budget are even smaller than those of some metropolitan and state ecumenical agencies. As the United Presbyterian Church's withdrawal and return suggested, many within the participating denominations view COCU with ambivalence.

A Costly Liberation

Part of the problem stems from the fact that COCU is bucking powerful cultural currents. For the many who have become disenchanted with all established institutions and prefer to "do their own thing" religiously, COCU is only a variation on the tired theme of organized religion. More traditional churchgoers resist the homogenizing pressures of modern mass society by reaffirming familiar ethnic and religious identities; the denominational home they know is more appealing to them than the "superchurch" they imagine. And even those who acknowledge a need for church union are prone to cast about for instant remedies and to regard with pessimism the prospects for major institutional change; they are inclined to tackle pressing short-range tasks and to forgo the more elusive long-range projects whose outcome is uncertain.

At the root of COCU's vulnerability is its primary objective: the transformation of the denominational system by which American Christians have traditionally organized their corporate religious life. This delicate flower called COCU not only challenges denominational structures; it also calls into question certain attitudes and modes of behavior long associated with those structures. The denominational system both supports and is supported by the deepest cleavages in American society; hence the radical changes sought by COCU would be of historic significance.

. . COCU is moving in response to an emerging vision of how the unity and diversity of the Christian community can best be expressed. This vision is, I believe, more faithful to the gospel and more responsive to humanity's needs than is the flawed vision served by denominational Christianity. The goal is a new church in which diverse Christian people are reconciled in Christ, but it is a goal that will not be realized until these Christians are liberated from features of the denominational system that foster estrangement. The reconciliation COCU seeks is elusive because that liberation is costly.

Fortunately for COCU the grip of the denominational system has begun to loosen—especially in Africa and Asia, where the most significant church unions have taken place and where the greatest number of current union negotiations are in progress. Organic unity has been more readily achieved in the Third World because the imported denominational system never became as entangled there with the structures of the larger society as it did in its North Atlantic homelands. . . .

COCU's search for a union of denominations involves considerably more than ecclesiastical machinery. It strikes at key problems in American life at the points where they are most deeply entrenched. Especially significant for COCU is the active presence of the African Methodist Episcopal Church, the African Methodist Episcopal Zion Church, and the Christian Methodist Episcopal Church. These three predominantly black churches have made it clear that they are not interested in a union that deals with racism in token ways. The reconciliation of black and white Christians in a united church can come only through the process of freeing them from structures, attitudes and behavior that have been instruments of oppression.

Because religious racism in the United States is so entwined with the denominational system, any far-reaching liberation from racism can be achieved only in conjunction with liberation from the denominational system itself. And that deliverance could bring a rich harvest in other realms as well where the denominational system still shapes us. . . .

At its Cincinnati plenary the Consultation took the first steps toward implementing the decision reached the pre-

vious year that it must return to basics before the participating churches will be ready for a fruitful consideration of
union blueprints. That decision requires a slower pace
toward union than was envisaged in the 1960s, but it should
prove wise if it allows COCU to pursue all implications of
the demanding vision it is attempting to serve.

The major lines of this more deliberate process became
evident during the Cincinnati plenary. The body determined that COCU's efforts on behalf of a reconstructed
Christian community should be based upon shared percep-
tions of such fundamental ecclesial realities as baptism and
the Lord's Supper. The delegates' decision to recommend
to their respective governing bodies the mutual recognition of members was grounded in the Consultation's long-
standing agreement that "all who are baptized into Christ
are members of his universal church and belong to and
share in his ministry."

Mutual recognition should lead to additional moves toward unity among the covenanted denominations: (1) participation and leadership by members of one church in
another; (2) an end to practices whereby one church inten-
tionally enlarges its membership at the expense of another;
(3) increased exploration of new possibilities for the
mutual recognition of the ordained ministries of both men
and women; and (4) intensified pursuit of union in a
Church of Christ Uniting.

Delegates to the plenary also agreed that if a future
united church is to overcome racial injustice, COCU denominations must recognize that racism has brought dep-
rivation to white and black, oppressor and oppressed alike.
Hence plans were initiated for "two-way compensatory action" intended (1) to help white churches learn from the
rich insights into the gospel that have emerged from oppressed minority churches and (2) to help black churches
develop programs and facilities that draw upon the resources of the white churches.

The Consultation also reaffirmed its intention to encourage groups from COCU denominations to form inclu-

sive local "generating communities" to experiment with
corporate patterns that work toward the goals to which
COCU is committed. Although only four such communities have been established since the 1973 plenary, more are
anticipated. . . . COCU's long-range credibility and effectiveness hinge largely upon the responsiveness of its eventual union models to signals received from such grass-
roots experimentation.

In such ways this "delicate flower" is pushing through
the ground. The process is slow; a long winter may lie
ahead. But the hopes of COCU's advocates should not be
discounted, for their vision rests upon solid foundations.

PROGRESS TOWARD CHRISTIAN UNIFICATION [4]

Not long ago, a commission of U.S. Lutheran and
Roman Catholic theologians wound up a three-year study
of Papal authority with a startling conclusion. Catholics,
they reported in substance, over-claimed when they said
that Christ appointed Peter as the first Pope, but Protestants have failed to acknowledge that a chief overseer is
needed. Nothing in the Bible, they said, prohibits Christians from designating one of their ministers to seek the
unity of all Christians.

A little earlier, a commission of Anglican and Catholic
theologians, after reviewing the great Reformation debate
over whether during the communion service Christ is
physically present in the bread and wine, came to the conclusion that what counts is the real presence of Christ in
the hearts of the participants.

Two more momentous developments could not be
imagined in the wave of religious tolerance set off by the
late Pope John XXIII's decision to convene the Second
Vatican Council in 1962—with observers in attendance
from nearly all branches of Christendom. Today, religious

[4] Excerpt from "What Progress Toward Church Reunion?" by James Daniel,
roving editor. Reader's Digest. 106:108–12. Ja. '75. Reprinted by permission.

détente has gone far indeed, and Christians are close to agreeing on many essentials.

Top-Level Convergence

Whether the winding down of 450 years of religious cold war portends one church, however, is debatable. Nine American denominations, with a membership of 24 million, noticeably backed away in the early 1970s from a plan of reunion. In their enthusiasm, the churchmen who devised the so-called COCU (Consultation on Church Union) plan for combining existing congregations into parishes with common property and shared ministers apparently got too far ahead of their rank and file. Yet even those churches that would not join COCU in the beginning increasingly talk of some ultimate form of reunion growing out of gradual convergences in belief and practice. [See the preceding article in this section, "Consultation on Church Union."]

If reunion comes, the result will bear little resemblance to the old-style military-chain-of-command kind of church policy. Even recent Vatican statements on ecumenism have begun to sound the cautionary note that any new association of churches must allow each religious community to preserve its "spiritual patrimony"—and must not be brought about by reducing everybody to the least common denominator of doctrine. Yet, 49 of the 169 Roman Catholic dioceses in this country now are full members of local councils of churches (up from one just five years ago), and there is serious speculation that before too long the National Conference of Catholic Bishops will affiliate with the National Council of Churches of Christ in America. In many places, the local councils have converted themselves into "associations" of Protestants, Catholics and Orthodox Christian churches, even taking new names.

Five years ago, for example, the Council of Churches of the Pittsburgh Area disbanded and reorganized as Christian Associates of Southwest Pennsylvania, representing 1.7

million Christians in nine counties and 2300 congregations. Frankly recognizing that there are still many areas
where churches want to go their separate ways, Christian
Associates concentrates on those "things we can do together that we cannot do alone."

Innovative approaches have ranged from professionally
produced radio and TV shows on religion to workshops
where 1500 lay teachers of religion have been coached by
professional educators in how to interest children and
adults in their faith. . . .

In a few places, the church councils now include Jews.
In Connecticut, Stamford, Darien, Greenwich and New
Canaan are served by a Council of Churches and Synagogues, which operates a housing project, an inner-city
day camp, a hospital chaplaincy service, a workshop where
psychiatrists advise ministers how to treat individuals or
families disrupted by divorce. The Council, with two other
groups, also established a community "re-entry" program
which has helped 200 released prisoners find places to live
and jobs in the past year and a half (with only three re-
convictions).

Prototypes for the Future

Many churches, particularly in the inner cities, are finding that they can survive only if they join forces. In Kansas City, Mo., one Presbyterian church was down to 50
congregants, mostly elderly women. A nearby congregation
of the United Church of Christ had a similar problem. "All
of a sudden," according to one church member, "the idea
hit us: Why are we working from—and paying for—two separate church buildings?" Once the decision was made to
combine forces, nearby Catholics and Episcopalians asked
for and received permission to hold their services with the
other two congregations. Today there is a new $400,000
building offering Mass at 9 A.M. and a combined Protestant
service at 11. The current head pastor, the Rev. Samuel E.
Mann, a Methodist, has remarked, "Even five years later,

around 300 visitors a year come to the church to study what we have done."

In the suburbs, too, where adults often sleep late Sunday morning or gear their Sunday lives to a country club, churches find that they must pull together or disappear apart. Consider Columbia, Md., between Washington and Baltimore, a huge "new town" that arose as a unit with shopping center, light industry, offices and square miles of houses. To meet religious needs, Columbia formed a Religious Facilities Corporation, which built a $1 million multiple-denomination church building. Its 23,000 square feet of usable space includes conference rooms often used for Sunday-school classes and nursery, pastors' studies, worship halls and lounges now used by four Christian and three Jewish congregations. A second such "religious facility" is under construction.

Reston, Va., another "new town," took a slightly different tack. When United Redeemer Methodist became firmly rooted there, the Christian Church (Disciples of Christ), United Church of Christ, the United Presbyterian Church and the Presbyterian Church of the United States —rather than compete with it for members—joined it to form the United Christian Parish of Reston, which now has two centers of worship and plans four eventually. The ministers rotate between the two worship centers, one of which is characterized by an informal style to appeal to younger members. As a prototype for future, wider reunion, each parish member is regarded as a member in full standing of all five of the sponsoring denominations.

Quarrels Contained

So far, however, inter-church cooperation has for the most part stopped short of the altar rail. Many Protestant churches, as well as the Catholic, do not practice "open communion" because they believe that to be meaningful it should express agreement of the partakers on a wide range of theological questions. Nonetheless, Catholics in several areas have lately set guidelines permitting their clergy to give communion in special circumstances to non-Catholics —*i.e.*, if the latter sincerely request it, understand it, and cannot be served by their own ministers.

Meanwhile, in the recent movement called "church in the home," free-form religious communities have been holding services of prayer and communion in living rooms. Mindful that Christianity began in the homes of humble working people, the churches have tried to stabilize, without discouraging, these movements. Catholic bishops often appoint a young, long-haired priest to work with members turned off by the Establishment, and the Presbyterians are experimenting with forming groups of home churches which report to a presbytery.

A distinct "plus" in the movement toward church re-union is an increase in good manners and a decrease in petty inter-church quarrels. One area where common courtesy was long overdue was in what used to be called "mixed marriage." In Massachusetts, a statewide Commission on Christian Unity, representing, among others, four Catholic dioceses and also Baptists, Episcopalians, United Methodists, Lutherans and United Church of Christ, has published new guidelines for what are now called "ecumenical marriages." Entitled "Living the Faith You Share," the guidelines urge these couples to worship *together* from time to time, to educate their children ecumenically and to conduct home worship. The Episcopal diocese advised its clergy: "We must not make the couple feel guilty of falling in love, when in fact the churches are guilty of the sin of separation."

The day when all baptized persons may be able to worship together comfortably has undoubtedly been hastened by widespread reforms in the liturgy. In this movement, the aim is to go behind the ceremonies frozen in the elaborate styles of the Reformation and Renaissance eras to the more austere forms of the early church. Catholics have had to accustom themselves to the most drastic changes. Not only have they dropped Latin; also, they have limited the number of universal saints' feast days. In addition, the Scriptural portions of the Mass have been increased and the communion portion abbreviated and rewritten until it differs little from many Protestant services.

On their side, the Protestants have hacked away at liturgical deadwood. In many places, Episcopalians no longer feast their ears on the sonorities of the Book of Common Prayer's version of Morning Prayer and Communion, but instead follow their own versions of the new liturgy. There is also a proposed common liturgy for communion, baptism and marriage devised by scholars and churchmen for the nine denominations still part of COCU....

Impossible Dream

The Vatican Council decree on ecumenism saw the task of reconciling Christians as "transcending human energies and abilities" and therefore to be accomplished only under Divine Providence. Some ecumenists think that it will take a terrible scourge, a cataclysm of some sort. Others hope that the difficulties the churches seem to be having in holding their members and clergy, the deterioration in the quality of society around them, will increasingly make Christians more conscious of their likenesses than of their differences. They look on membership losses as resulting in fewer but more dedicated Christians who will be more effective.

At a recent Catholic-Baptist conference in Daytona Beach, Fla., Cecil Sherman, pastor of the Asheville, N.C., First Baptist Church, said God is "saving the church" even now. "He is remaking it. It will be smaller, but it will be more lean for the long pull. It will not be so gaudy in wealth, but it will have more of the pungency of saving salt."

Dr. Sherman remarked that the "growing secularity of our time" was driving Southern Baptists (12.5 million strong, but not yet part of the Council of Churches) and Catholics (once felt by some Southern Baptists to be condemned to hell or "saved in spite of their church") toward each other. "A secular world cannot tell the difference between us. If a secular world considers the two of us as Christian, might we not do ourselves a favor to consider each other as Christian and pool our resources where we can? 'To save the world' by Christian definitions is a large order, and even God may need both of us to get the job done."

BIBLIOGRAPHY

An asterisk (*) preceding a reference indicates that the article or a part of it has been reprinted in this book.

BOOKS, PAMPHLETS, AND DOCUMENTS

Ahlstrom, S. E. A religious history of the American people. Yale University Press. '72.

American Theological Library Association. Index to religious periodical literature. The Association. 7301 Germantown Ave. Philadelphia, PA 19119.
Issued semiannually.

*Council on Religion and International Affairs. Worldview symposium on the Hartford appeal. The Council. 170 E. 64th St. New York, NY 10021. '75.
Reprinted in this book: An appeal for theological affirmation. p 3–4.

Cox, H. G. The seduction of the spirit; the use and misuse of people's religion. Simon & Schuster. '73.

Fine, Morris and others, eds. American Jewish year book, 1977. Jewish Publication Society of America. 117 S. 17th St. Suite 2300. Philadelphia, PA 19103. '76.

Garrison, O. V. The hidden story of scientology. Arlington Books. '74. [Distributed in USA by Citadel Press.]

Greeley, A. M. The American Catholic. Basic Books. '77.

Greenfield, Robert. The spiritual supermarket. Saturday Review Press. '75.

*Hudson, W. S. Religion in America; an historical account of development of American religious life. Scribner. '73.

Johnson, Paul. A history of Christianity. Atheneum. '76.

Kaufmann, Walter. Religion in four dimensions. Reader's Digest Press. '76.

Martin, Malachi. The new castle; reaching for the ultimate. Dutton. '74.

Mead, F. S. Handbook of denominations in the United States. new 6th ed. Abingdon. '75.

Miller, D. L. The new polytheism; rebirth of the gods and goddesses. Harper. '74.

Nielsen, N. C. Jr. The religion of President Carter. Thomas Nelson. '77.

Richardson, H. V. Dark salvation; the story of Methodism as it developed among blacks in America. Doubleday. '76.

Rosten, L. C. ed. Religions of America; ferment and faith in an age of crisis; a new guide and almanac. Simon & Schuster. '75.

Routtenberg, M. J. The decades of decision. Bloch. '73.
Snook, J. B. Going further; life-and-death religion in America. Prentice-Hall. '73.
Strober, G. S. American Jews: community in crisis. Doubleday. '74.
Ward, H. H. The far-out saints of the Jesus communes; a first-hand report and interpretation of the Jesus people movement. Association Press. '72.
Ward, H. H. Religion 2101 A.D. Doubleday. '75.
Washington, J. R. Jr. Black sects and cults. (C. Eric Lincoln Series on Black Religion) Doubleday. '72.
*Wells, D. F. and Woodbridge, J. D. eds. The evangelicals; what they believe, who they are, where they are changing. Abingdon. '75.
Yearbook of American and Canadian churches, 1977. C. H. Jacquet Jr. ed. Abingdon. '77.
Zaretsky, I. I. and Leone, M. P. eds. Religious movements in contemporary America. Princeton University Press. '74.

PERIODICALS

* Africa. No 50:60-1+. O. '75. Abdul Farrakhan, minister, nation of Islam; interview. Howard Lee.
*America. 131:111-13. S. 14, '74. Why are parochial schools closing? S. F. Overlan.
America. 132:334-7. My. 3, '75. Finding God and the Hartford appeal. Avery Dulles.
America. 136:118-19. F. 12, '77. Women's ordination: the future of equality.
America. 136:146-8. F. 19, '77. Reconciliation in Memphis: a diocese prepared. Albert Kirk.
America. 136:438-40. My. 14, '77. "Moonies"—religious converts or psychic victims? R. A. Walsh.
American Scholar. 45:499-518. Autumn '76. The Protestant establishment revisited. E. D. Baltzell.
American Sociological Review. 41:195-208. Ap. '76. Traditional religion in contemporary society: a theory of local-cosmopolitan plausibility. W. C. Roof.
Arts in Society. 13:10-191. Spring/Summer '76. Religious communities and the arts. [special issue]
Business and Society Review. No 16:68-9. Winter '75-'76. Church and capitalism—an old struggle. J. W. Fraser.
Center Magazine. 7:8-10. S. '74. Religion and revolution. Harvey Wheeler.
Center Magazine. 7:47-57+. N. '74. Culture and religion. Milton Singer.

*Christian Century. 92:83-6. Ja. 29, '75. Postdenominational church: will COCU's [Consultation on Church Union] delicate flower blossom? P. M. Minus Jr.

Christian Century. 92:326-7. Ap. 2 '75. Episcopal controversy; ordination of women.

Christian Century. 92:568-72. Je. 4, '75. Ecumenism's past and future: shifting perspectives [interview with S. C. Neill]. J. E. Groh.

*Christian Century. 92:1133-7. D. 10, '75. Secular selling of a religion. G. E. La More Jr.

Christian Century. 93:997-8. N. 17, '76. Catholic hopes and fears; Call to Action conference in Detroit.

Christian Century. 93:1165-6. D. 29, '76. 1976: the year of the evangelical.

Christian Century. 94:405-7. Ap. 27, '77. Dominance syndrome. J. M. Luecke.

Christianity and Crisis. 35:12-16. F. 3, '75. Churches and world hunger. Milo Thornberry.

Christianity and Crisis. 35:168-79. Jl. 21, '75. Hartford debate. R. J. Neuhaus and others.

*Christianity and Crisis. 36:23-7. F. 16, '76. Boston affirmations.

Christianity and Crisis. 36:173-5. Jl. 19, '76. Rev. Moon and his Bicentennial blitz. James Stentzel.

Christianity and Crisis. 32:264-6. N. 15, '76. Did Detroit really happen? the U.S. Catholic bishops' conference. Joe Cunneen.

Christianity and Crisis. 37:36-7. Mr. 7, '77. Vatican on women priests. R. G. Hoyt.

Christianity Today. 19:55-6. S. 12, '75. Episcopal revolt; the ordination of women issue.

Christianity Today. 21:48-52. O. 8, '76. Episcopal church: women are winners; adoption of modern-language prayer book. E. E. Plowman.

Christianity Today. 21:58-60. N. 5, '76. Jewish challenge at the NCC. A. H. Matthews.

Christianity Today. 21:12-16. D. 3, '76. How Christian is America? C. P. Wagner.

Christianity Today. 21:16-17. My. 20, '77. Is America over-evangelized? D. W. Hillis.

Christianity Today. 21:42-3. My. 20, '77. Episcopalians: words of caution.

*Clearing House. 48:356-60. F. '74. Religion: an integral part of public education. J. H. Krahn.

Commentary. 57:49-52. Ja. '74. That old-time religion. James Hitchcock.

Commonweal. 102:617-23. D. 19, '75. Church of the future; excerpt from the runaway church. Peter Hebblethwaite.

Commonweal. 103:746-8. N. 19, '76. Made in Detroit; Catholic conference on liberty and justice for all. T. C. Fox.

Commonweal. 103:807-16. D. 17, '76. Women in the church [3 articles]. Francine Cardman; Lois Spear; Michael Novak.

Commonweal. 104:38-9. Ja. 21, '77. Reconciliation in Memphis. R. R. Holton.

Commonweal. 104:109-12. F. 18, '77. More on women in the church.

* Congressional Digest. 53:3-9+. Ja. '74. Congress and the school prayer controversy.

Critic. 33:14-21. Ja. '75. American Catholics—ten years later. A. M. Greeley and others.

Critic. 34:58-66. Spring '76. Catholic left: an elegy of sorts. John Deedy.

Critic. 34:14-47+. Summer '76. Catholicism in America: two hundred years and counting; a personal interpretation. A. M. Greeley.

Critic. 35:14-26. Fall '76. Uncertain church: the new Catholic problem. G. A. Kelly.

* Ebony. 32:75-6+. N. '76. Ship of AME Zion rides a freedom tide. Martin Weston.

*Editorial Research Reports. v 2 no 8:563-80. Ag. 8, '75. Year of religion. H. B. Shaffer.

Editorial Research Reports. v 2, no 8:623-40. Ag. 27, '76. Politics and religion. H. B. Shaffer.

* Fortune. 91:134-5+. Ap. '75. Battered pillars of the American system: religion. P. L. Berger.

Fortune. 93:222-5+. My. '76. There's an unholy mess in the churchly economy. James Gollin.

Geographical Review. 66:420-34. O. '76. Patterns of religion in the United States. J. R. Shortridge.

Harper's Magazine. 249:20-4+. D. '74. Raise your hand if you're an eternal spirit soul; Hare Krishna movement. Judith Wax.

Harvard Educational Review. 44:411-40. Ag. '74. America in search of a new ideal; an essay on the rise of pluralism. William Greenbaum.

* Humanist. 37:36-43, Ja./F.; 38-9+, Mr./Ap. '77. The resurgence of fundamentalism; a symposium.
   Reprinted in this book: A dynamic religious diversity. E. L. Ericson. p 37, Ja./F. '77; Criticizing religious beliefs. Walter Kaufmann. p 42—3. Mr./Ap. '77.

Intellect. 104:171-4. N. '75. Occult today: why? G. E. Kessler.

Intellect. 104:535-8. Ap. '76. Religion and the future; an overview. L. J. Putnam.

Intellect. 105:163-7. D. '76. What's going on in religious education? N. H. Thompson.

Interpretation. 30:36-43. Ja. '76. Some musings on a nation under God. Gardner Taylor.

Interpretation. 30:44-51. Ja. '76. Space and time in American religious experience. Joseph Sittler.

*Journal of Current Social Issues. 14:50-5. Spring '77. U.S. in early stage of religious revival? George Gallup Jr.

Journal of Social Issues, v 30, no 3:23-42. '74. Jesus people movement: a generational interpretation. Jack Balswick.

Midstream. 20:47-66. Ag./S. '74. American Jews and the Protestant community. G. S. Strober.

Modern Age. 18:163-74. Spring '74. Institutional church and political activity. R. de V. Williamson.

* National Review. 26:926-8. Ag. 16, '74. Religion: all quiet on the western front. M. B. Martin.

*National Review. 28:840-2. Ag. 6, '76. Severed roots of American Christianity. Paul Williams.

* National Review. 27:1171-2+. O. 29, '76. Sociological "religion" versus Christianity. J. J. Lynch.

National Review. 28:1348-9. D. 10, '76. Mice that roared; Call to Action conference in Detroit. Russell Kirk.

Nation's Business. 63:16. F. '75. Prayer in the schools: an overwhelming verdict.

New Catholic World. 219:98+. My. '76. Ethnicity in the church; symposium.

New Catholic World. 219:155-9. Jl. '76. How Americans look at religion today; civil religion. M. A. Neal.

New Republic. 171:33-41. N. 23, '74. New religious consciousness. R. N. Bellah.

New York Times. p 1 Jl. 12, '76. Clergy rallying to social causes. K. A. Briggs.

*New York Times. sec IV, p 22. Ja. 9, '77. Catholic bishops in the U.S. no longer speak in a single voice. K. A. Briggs.

New York Times. p A 8. Ja. 28, '77. Excerpts from Vatican's declaration affirming prohibition on women priests.

*New York Times. p A 25. F. 16, '77. Playing the devil's advocate, as it were. Harvey Cox.

New York Times. p A 12. Mr. 25, '77. Ordination of women is supported by federation of Catholic priests.

New York Times. p 8. Ap. 9, '77. Religious "brainwashing" dispute. K. A. Briggs.

New York Times. p 36. Ap. 17, '77. Evangelistic drive intensifies and so does debate about it. K. A. Briggs.

New York Times. p 42. Ap. 26, '77. Spiritual renewal among Jews noted. K. A. Briggs.

New York Times. p A 14. Ap. 29, '77. Report finds evangelical churches continue to grow as others decline. K. A. Briggs.

New York Times. p D 23. My. 4, '77. Conservative Judaism approves 2-year study on ordaining women.

New York Times. sec IV, p 18. Je. 5, '77. Some scholars believe Vatican III a necessity. K. A. Briggs.

*New York Times. p A 15. Je. 22, '77. New religious movements considered likely to last. K. A. Briggs.

*New York Times. p B 1. Jl. 22, '77. "Charismatic Christians" seek to infuse the faith with their joyous spirit. K. A. Briggs.

* New York Times Magazine. p 16-17. My. 16, '76. There are no churches for atheists. Walter Goodman.

New York Times Magazine. p 6-7+. Je. 27, '76. To march or not to march; the Hartford statement and the Boston affirmations. Francine du Plessix.

New York Times Magazine. p 8-9+. Ag. 1, '76. "Born again" politics. Gary Wills.

New York Times Magazine. p 16+. O. 10, '76. Violence of "just sitting" [Zen Buddhism]. Lawrence Shainberg.

New York Times Magazine. p 9+. Ja. 16, '77. Divided shepherds of a restive flock. T. J. Fleming.

* Newsweek. 86:64. S. 29, '75. New heretics, second Hartford conference. S. C. Cowley and Laurie Lisle.

* Newsweek. 88:68-70+. O. 25, '76. Born again! K. L. Woodward and others.

* Newsweek. 88:110-11. N. 8, '76. Speaking up; national assembly of Roman Catholics in Detroit. K. L. Woodward and J. C. Jones.

* Newsweek. 89:85. Ja. 17, '77. Women ordained. Margaret Montagno and Laurie Lisle.

Psychology Today. 8:131-6. N. '74. Shifting focus of faith; a survey report. Robert Wuthnow and C. Y. Glock.

* Reader's Digest. 106:108-12. Ja. '75. What progress toward church reunion? James Daniel.

Redbook. 148:126-7+. Ap. '77. 65,000 women reveal how religion affects health, happiness, sex and politics. Claire Safran.

Religion in Life. 43:175-82. Summer '74. Instant everything. S. T. Kimbrough Jr.

Religion in Life. 44:24-35. Spring '75. Civil religion in America. D. S. Ross.

Religion in Life. 44:93-104. Spring '75. What does it mean to be Protestant? N. E. Dunkle.

Religion in Life. 45:41-52. Spring '76. Supreme Court's three tests of the Establishment clause. R. B. Flowers.

Religion in Life. 45:308-17. Autumn '76. Present and future of theology. Kenneth Cauthen.

Religion in Life. 45:468-76. Winter '76. American civil religion and hermeneutics. Barbara Engler.

* Saturday Review. 2:6. Jl. 12, '75. Ferment in our churches. Leo Rosten.

* Saturday Review. 4:10-11. Je. 25, '77. Confusion among the faithful. M. E. Marty.

Senior Scholastic. 109:38-41. S. 23, '76. Judaism.

Senior Scholastic. 109:10-12. D. 16, '76. Roman Catholicism.

* Senior Scholastic. 109:22-4+. Ap. 7, '77. Protestantism.

* Seventeen. 34:96-7+. Jl. '75. Why are teens turning to religion? Kenneth Woodward and Elizabeth Woodward.

Social Forces. 53:581-94. Je. '75. Christian beliefs, nonreligious factors, and anti-Semitism. D. R. Hoge and J. W. Carroll.

Social Forces. 54:890-900. Je. '76. Civil religious dimension: is it there? R. C. Wimberley and others.

Sociological Quarterly. 16:162-70. Spring '75. Conversion in a Billy Graham crusade: spontaneous event or ritual performance? R. C. Wimberley and others.

Theology Today. 32:175-82. Jl. '75. Civil religion and the churches behaving civilly. M. E. Marty.

Thought. 51:123-34. Je. '76. Catholic laity and the charismatic renewal: is this the reformation? J. H. Fichter.

* Time. 107:50. Ja. 19, '76. Counterattack, Boston industrial mission's response to Hartford conference.

* Time. 107:48-50+. My. 24, '76. Church divided.

* U.S. News & World Report. 61:90-2+. S. 26, '66. Church in the news: story of Mormon success.

U.S. News & World Report. 78:47-9. Mr. 17, '75. Religion and science: working together to close the gaps.

* U.S. News & World Report. 79:53-6. Ag. 18, '75. Comeback for religion in the schools?

* U.S. News & World Report. 79:56. Ag. 18, '75. Prayer in schools —still a troubling issue.

* U.S. News & World Report. 80:52-4. Je. 14, '76. Religious cults: newest magnet for youth.

U.S. News & World Report. 81:25-6. Jl. 19, '76. Southern Baptists —who they are, what they believe.

* U.S. News & World Report. 82:54-8+. Ap. 11, '77. Time of renewal for U.S. churches.

* Village Voice. 21:11-13. Ag. 16, '76. An ex-believer defends Carter's religion. Robert Christgau.

Virginia Quarterly Review. 51:161-85. Spring '75. Great re-awakening. H. S. Ashmore.

Vital Speeches of the Day. 42:149-55. D. 15, '75. Political action
    for liberty and justice in education; address, October 30, 1975.
    V. C. Blum.
Washington Monthly. 7:21-30. O. '75. Liberal plot to kill God.
    Walter Shapiro.
Yale Review. 65:203-17. Winter '76. The religious crisis of our
    culture. Louis Dupré.